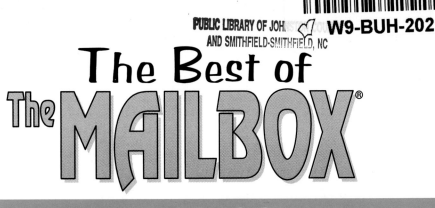

THE BEST OF The MAILBOX® Magazine

The Best of The MAILBOX®

PRESCHOOL

Since the first book published in 1993, **The Best of** The **Mailbox**® books have become the most popular titles available to teachers of early learners. Now we're proud to present the newest **The Best of The Mailbox**® book—just for preschool teachers! Inside these covers, you'll find many of the best teacher-tested ideas published in the 1995–1999 issues of **The Preschool Mailbox**® magazine. These practical ideas were selected from those sent to us by teachers across the United States and Canada. We've included thematic units as well as many of our regularly featured departments.

www.themailbox.com

Editor:
Jayne Gammons

Artist:
Teresa R. Davidson

Cover Artist:
Kimberly Richard

©2000 by THE EDUCATION CENTER, INC.
All rights reserved.
ISBN# 1-56234-367-X

Manufactured in the United States
10 9 8 7 6 5 4 3 2 1

Table Of Contents

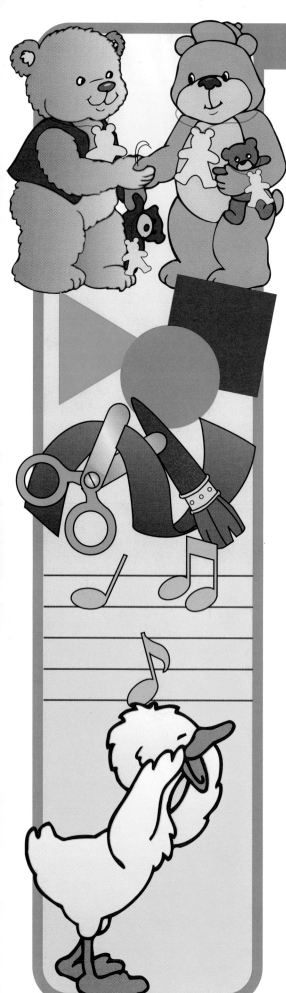

THEME UNITS

Teddy Bears Go To School

Give a warm-and-fuzzy welcome to your preschool pals. With this collection of activities, your classroom will soon be filled with teddy bear friends, teddy bear hugs, and teddy bear learning fun!

ideas by Pamela K. Priest

A Warm-And-Fuzzy Welcome

Any feelings of uncertainty about the first day of school will "bearly" be visible if you invite your little ones to bring along a familiar friend—a teddy bear. Several weeks before the first day of school, prepare an invitation to send to each child. Duplicate the invitation on page 9 onto colorful paper so that the illustration is on the top half of the paper. Fold the pages so that the invitations resemble cards. On each card write a different child's name and the name of your own teddy bear. Ask a friend to take a picture of you holding a teddy bear. Once you have the negative of the picture, order a class supply of duplicates. Mount a picture inside each child's card; then sign the card, "Your teacher and teddy bear friend, [your name] and [your teddy's name]." After you have addressed the envelopes, send the cards on their way and wait patiently for that special first day!

Making Memories

Keep a camera handy during the first teddy bear days. You'll want to capture the fun on film to complete the "Teddy Bear Annual" described on page 8.

Teddy Bear Talk

Prior to the first day of school, prepare matching nametags for each child and her bear. From tan construction paper, cut a bear shape for each child and a miniature bear shape for each child's bear. Personalize each child's nametag; then punch a hole near the top of each student and bear nametag. Pair a bear's nametag with each personalized nametag; then divide them into four groups. Using a different color of ribbon for each group, thread a ribbon through each nametag.

As youngsters arrive at your door on the first day, greet them with a hug from your own teddy bear. (Use the same bear shown in the photo included in your invitation.) Tie each child's nametag and place it around her neck. On a bear nametag with the same color of ribbon, write the name of the child's bear. Tie it around the bear's neck.

When every child has arrived, gather them together at your group area. Talk about the color of ribbon on each bear's nametag. Then encourage your little ones to find other teddy bears with the same color of ribbon. Ask the children to help the matching teddies say, "Hello." Who says teddy bears can't talk?

Dear ___Ben___,

Welcome to preschool! We're going to have tons of teddy bear fun. Please bring a teddy bear to preschool with you on your first day. Don't forget to name your bear.

Open this card to see a picture of me with my bear, ___Bobo___.

Your teacher and teddy bear friend, Ms. Priest and Bobo

Teddy Bear, Teddy Bear

Everyone loves to chant—even teddy bears! Teach your little ones the following rhyme to help them learn their new preschool pals' names. Seat the children—and their teddy bears—in a group on the floor. Ask a volunteer to stand up with his teddy bear. Chant the rhyme with the rest of the class, using the child's and his teddy bear's names. Continue until each child has had an opportunity to stand.

As students gain knowledge of their new friends' names, try this variation. Seat the children in a circle on the floor. Ask a volunteer to stand in the middle of the circle with his teddy bear. As a class chant the first line of the rhyme while the child in the center walks around the circle. Direct the child in the center to select another child from the group and to say the second line of the rhyme, filling in the selected child and his bear's name.

Teddy Bear, Teddy Bear, whom do you see?
I see [child's name] and [bear's name] looking at me!

Let's Go, Teddies!

Leaving home to go to preschool each morning is no big deal when you have a teddy to take with you. This get-acquainted movement song will help youngsters get excited about getting up and getting ready. Seat the class in a row on the floor. Place each child's teddy bear in a row facing the children. Ask the children to pretend it's time to get ready to go to school and remind them that they should take their teddies with them. Sing the following song, inserting a child's name where appropriate. Ask that child to jump up, hold his teddy by the arm, and join you in line by holding your hand. Continue to sing the song until every child has had an opportunity to get his bear and join the line by holding the paw of the child's bear whose name was previously sung. When the children and bears are all in the line, lead them in skipping around the room. Ready, Teddy? Let's go!

Going To Preschool
(sung to the tune of "Down By The Station")

Going to preschool, early in the morning.
See all the teddy bears sitting in a row.
See [child's name] grab [his/her] little teddy.
Jump up, skip, skip. [Child's name], let's go!

Teddy Bear Tour

While you have your preschoolers and their teddies lined up, why not take a stroll around your school so everyone can get their bearings? Lead a teddy bear tour to the important locations in your school such as the director's office and the cafeteria. Using a Polaroid® camera, take pictures of the school personnel you meet along the way. Later, during a group time, discuss the people in the pictures. Give your preschoolers practice learning these new names and faces by saying the "Teddy Bear, Teddy Bear" chant above as you show each picture.

Mrs. Desimone
Cook

How To Get
Your "Bear" Share

Teddy bears know how to be the "beary" best of friends. After learning this action rhyme, your little ones will, too! Assure the children that even though they will share their bears during this activity, every bear will be returned to its original owner when the fun is over.

Teddy Bear Hugs

Teddy bear hugs   *Hug bear.*
Are eyes that see,   *Point to bear's eyes.*
Ears that listen   *Point to bear's ears.*
To you and me.   *Point to another and self.*

Teddy bear hugs   *Hug bear.*
Are hands that share,   *Point to bear's paws.*
Arms for helping   *Hold out bear's arms.*
To show you care.   *Smile at bear.*

Teddy bear hugs   *Hug bear.*
Are from the heart.   *Point to bear's chest.*
So be like a teddy—   *Put nose on bear's nose.*

A friend from the start.   *Share bear with a friend and repeat rhyme.*

fuzzy
gentle
quiet
warm
kind

The Beary Best Bears

Teddy Bear Time

When a child is bearing more resemblance to a grizzly bear than a teddy bear, use this positive approach to help her get back on the right track. During a group time, assist youngsters in describing the lovable characteristics of a teddy bear using words such as *fuzzy, gentle, quiet, warm,* and *kind.* Write the youngsters' descriptive words and phrases on a large bear shape cut from bulletin-board paper. Discuss with your little ones ways they can be more like a teddy bear. Post the chart in a small area of your room that has been designated as a "time-out"-only place. Place several teddy bears and other bear paraphernalia in the area as well. Then, when a child needs to be reminded to act more like a teddy, ask her to visit that area. After the appropriate amount of time, visit the child and use the bears to discuss the situation. When the teddy bear time is over, be sure to give the child a great big teddy bear hug!

Grin And Share It!

Grin and bear your show-and-tell time with this idea related to a favorite bear story—*A Pocket For Corduroy* by Don Freeman (Puffin Books). To prepare for show-and-tell, dress a tan teddy in overalls. If the overalls do not have a pocket, cut a felt pocket and glue it on. Cut a class supply plus one more of cards that will fit inside the pocket. Label one of the cards "CORDUROY" and place it in the bear's pocket. Label each of the remaining cards with a different child's name.

During a storytime, point out the card in the bear's pocket; then read aloud *A Pocket For Corduroy.* At the conclusion of the story, take the card from the bear's pocket and read the word *Corduroy.*

As often as you would like to have show-and-tell, place a child's card in the pocket. Give positive, descriptive clues about that child. When the children guess the child's name written on the card, take the card out of the pocket and give the bear to that child. Ask him to take the bear home and to put something special in the pocket. The next day, when the child returns the bear, encourage him to lead a guessing game about the object he brought to share.

What To Wear, Teddy Bear?

Give youngsters extra paws-on practice in going through a morning routine in order to get ready for school. In advance collect props such as a toothbrush, a comb, a washcloth, and other items that a child might use when getting ready for school in the morning. Also collect a wide variety of multi-seasonal baby or doll clothes.

Ask your little ones and their bears to join you for a teddy bear circle time. Display the props and clothing, and ask youngsters to share with you their morning routines. Describe different types of weather and ask youngsters to help you select the clothing that might be appropriate for a teddy to wear to school on each different type of day. Then place the props and clothing in a dramatic play area. Encourage youngsters who visit the center to pretend to assist their bears in getting ready for school. As each child dresses his bear in the provided clothing, encourage him to visit your painting center for the activity described in "Teddy Bear Takes A Pose."

Teddy Bear Takes A Pose

Youngsters who participate in "What To Wear, Teddy Bear?" will want to visit your painting center to paint school portraits of their teddy bears. Create a background for the portraits by placing school props such as crayons and scissors on a shelf near the area. Encourage each child to set her dressed bear on the shelf and to arrange the provided materials around the bear as desired. At a nearby easel (yet far enough away to avoid getting paint on the posed teddy), have her paint a portrait of her well-schooled bear. Write the name of the child's bear on the paper. When every child has had an opportunity to paint a masterpiece, bind the paintings between covers. Title the collection "Teddy Bears Go To School." Share the book during a group time; then display it in the art center for other aspiring artists. Ready, Teddy? Smile!

This is Freddy.

Amy

Teddy Bear Graduation

When the children are feeling comfortable in their new learning environment, celebrate by having a teddy bear graduation. Duplicate the teddy bear diploma on page 9 for each bear. Program each diploma with the appropriate information; then, on the back of each diploma, write the name of the child who will receive it. Roll each diploma so that the name is visible; then tie it with a length of yarn. To make a graduation cap for each bear, cut a five-inch square from black construction paper. Tie a knot at one end of a seven-inch piece of yarn. Tie the other end of the yarn to a brad; then insert the brad into the center of the paper square. To the underside of the cap, tape a rubber band for securing the cap on the bear's head.

On graduation day, present each child's bear with a diploma and secure the cap on its head. Take a picture of each graduating teddy and its owner to include in the "Teddy Bear Annual" (below). Serve teddy-bear-shaped crackers as a special treat. Explain to the children that since the teddy bears have officially graduated from preschool, they can begin staying at home. Wish the teddies good luck and congratulate the preschoolers on a terrific start!

Teddy Bear Annual

A teddy bear annual is the perfect way to introduce each child's family to the other children and teddies in the class. Compile the pictures taken during the activities of the first days of preschool into a scrapbook. Label each picture with the names of the children and teddies shown in the picture. Also include a brief description of the activity captured on film. Send the annual home with a different child every few nights. What a class!

The Bear Necessities

There are tons of teddy bear books available for reading aloud! These favorite titles are all about teddy bears and school.

Where Is The Bear At School?
Written by Bonnie Larkin Nims
Illustrated by Madelaine Gill

One Bear In The Picture
Written & Illustrated by Caroline Bucknall

My Brown Bear Barney
Written by Dorothy Butler
Illustrated by Elizabeth Fuller

Eddie And Teddy
Written & Illustrated by Gus Clarke

Dear _____,

Welcome to preschool! We're going to have tons of teddy bear fun. Please bring a teddy bear to preschool with you on your first day. Don't forget to name your bear.

Open this card to see a picture of me with my bear, _____.

name of bear

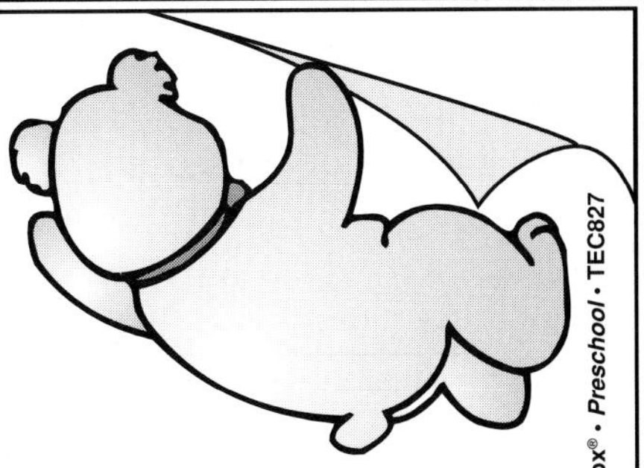

©The Education Center, Inc. • *The Best of* The Mailbox® • *Preschool* • TEC827

Teddy Bear Diploma
Use with "Teddy Bear Graduation" on page 8.

Teddy Bear Diploma

This certifies that _____ has "beary"

bear's name

successfully completed teddy bear preschool.

Graduation congratulations to _____!

child's name

_____
teacher

_____
school

_____
date

©The Education Center, Inc. • *The Best of* The Mailbox® • *Preschool* • TEC827

Happy Birthday!

Birthdays are so much fun, isn't it a shame they only last a day? Stretch a special day into a special week by adding festive touches to your classroom centers. The learning opportunities are sure to be cause for celebration!

ideas by dayle timmons

It's A Party And Everyone's Invited!

Turn your dramatic play area into party central. Purchase or have the children help you decorate a birthday banner. Suspend the banner over the area along with streamers and balloons. (Make sure that the balloons are out of little hands' reach.) Stock the center with birthday plates, cups, napkins, paper and crayons, gift-wrapped boxes, hats, and horns.

To make a permanent birthday cake for the center, spread plaster of Paris over the top and sides of a cake-shaped piece of Styrofoam®. Before the plaster sets, insert birthday candles or candleholders. Add decorative details to the cake with plaster that has been tinted with food coloring, or decorate the top of the cake with colored glue once the plaster is dry. If desired hot-glue fabric trims or beads to the base of the cake.

As children visit the center, seize the opportunity to reinforce math skills and language development as youngsters prepare invitations, set the birthday table, and more. What a celebration station!

Birthday Royalty

Everyone celebrating a birthday deserves to feel like a king or queen. If you're having a weeklong party, that includes everyone! Set up a birthday crown-making station at your art center for your birthday royalty. Cut crown shapes from wrapping paper or construction paper; then mount the shapes onto colorful sentence strips. Provide a variety of art supplies such as wrapping-paper scraps, metallic paper, sequins, jewels, glitter, colored glue, and scissors for decorating the crowns. Happy birthday, Your Majesty!

Creative Collages

Take a breath and make a birthday wish for the creation of creative collages. Stock an art center with geometric shapes cut from birthday-style wrapping paper. Also provide die-cut, birthday-related, construction-paper shapes; curling ribbon; birthday-related stickers; used birthday cards; large sheets of colorful construction paper; scissors; and glue. As students visit the art center, encourage them to use their choice of the provided materials to make a collage. Top each collage with a bow and personalized gift tag; then display it near the center.

Pam Crane

Play-Dough Party Place

Join the fun at the play-dough party place where birthday cakes are the focus of the fun. Collect disposable tart pans, potpie tins, and muffin pans. Place the pans in a center along with play dough, birthday candles or cut straws, craft sticks or plastic knives, and festive paper plates. Let's make a cake!

Birthday-Bash Splash

Adding candles to your water table will really take the cake! Ask parents to donate used candles in a variety of shapes, colors, and sizes. Next cut cake shapes from Styrofoam® meat trays. Using a permanent marker, label each cutout with a different numeral from one to five. As children visit the water table, encourage them to describe and compare the different types of candles. Ask them to predict whether the candles will sink or float. Then allow the students to enjoy free water play with the candles. Challenge youngsters to float a labeled cake cutout in the water and to place the corresponding number of candles on the cutout. How many candles will float on a cutout before it sinks or tips over? Does the size of the candle make a difference? This center is sure to be a birthday blowout!

Celebrate With Sand

As a variation to the "Play-Dough Party Place" (above), encourage youngsters to visit your sand table to "bake" a cake. Excluding the play dough, include all of the items previously suggested. In addition place mixing bowls and big spoons in the center. Also place a spray bottle filled with water in the center to keep the sand damp. Solicit sequential cake-baking directions from your little bakers. Ask, "How many scoops of sand are needed to make a cake? How many scoops are needed for a cupcake? Why does a sand cake need water?" At this birthday center, each discovery is sure to be a special event.

Make A Wish

If you'd like to add math opportunities to your birthday bonanza, then your wish has come true. Place a set of pegboards and pegs in a manipulative center. As a youngster places the pegs in the pegboard, encourage her to pretend she is putting candles on a cake. Have her "blow out" the candles; then sing the birthday song together. Challenge a youngster to put a specific number of peg candles on the pegboard cake or to put only candles that are a requested color. Assist the child in sorting the candles and in creating patterns.

Count On Fine-Motor Fun

Purchase colorful note pads in birthday-related shapes. Or cut out construction-paper birthday cake or cupcake shapes. Mount the shapes on tagboard; then laminate them for durability. To make counting games, label each cutout with a different numeral. Direct students to place the appropriate number of jumbo-sized birthday candles on each cutout.

To make lacing cards, trim around the shape of the laminated cutouts. Using a hole puncher, punch holes around the perimeter of the shape. Tie a knot at one end of a shoelace; then encourage a child to thread the lace through the shape.

The Icing On The Cake

For youngsters, making birthday cupcakes will be the icing on the cake of your birthday celebration. Divide the class into several small groups. Invite each group to visit your classroom cooking center to assist you in preparing cake batter. (Use any boxed cake mix or follow your favorite cake recipe. If desired add sprinkles to the batter.) Have each child spoon some batter into a personalized cupcake liner. When the cupcakes have been baked and are cool, provide each child with his cupcake, icing, and a craft stick. Have him ice his cupcake, then decorate it using small candies and candy sprinkles. When it's time to eat, give each child a candle to put in his cupcake. Have him make a wish, pretend to blow out the candle, and enjoy his treat. Happy birthday to me!

Happy Birthday To YOU!

Ideas For Making Each Child's Birthday Special

Birthday Bulletin Board

Spotlight your current birthday boy or girl with a bulletin board that has presence. Mount wrapping paper on a bulletin board; then add the title "Happy Birthday To You!" In advance of each child's birthday, send a note home requesting pictures of the child and other mountable items related to the child's interests. If possible feature each child during the week before or after her birthday. Assign a special week for students who have birthdays during the summer or school holidays. Be sure to provide time for the birthday boy or girl to discuss with the class the pictures and items chosen for display. Don't forget to include yourself during your own special week or feature yourself during Open House to introduce yourself to parents!

A Birthday Bundle

A take-home bundle is a bona fide way to thrill every birthday boy or girl. Fill a backpack, bookbag, large birthday gift bag, or decorated, handled plastic box with a collection of birthday goodies. Consider including some of these items:

- a birthday-related picture book (See the list at the right.)
- a videocassette of a birthday-related story
- a stuffed toy dressed in a vest or bandana made from festive fabric
- a recipe for a special birthday treat such as cookies or cupcakes
- birthday-party supplies such as noisemakers, birthday hats, and festive plates
- a goodie bag of small prizes
- crayons and a class birthday book (Bind blank paper between laminated wrapping-paper covers.)
  - a note to caregivers requesting that they assist the child in drawing a picture in the birthday book and record the child's dictated description of his special day

Request that the bundle of materials (excluding the goodie bag and party supplies) be returned after one week.

A Box Of Birthday Books

On or near each child's special day, request that he choose a book from a gift bag or gift-wrapped box of birthday-related titles. Read aloud his selection to the class. If desired, request that he hold the book as you read or that he assist you in retelling the story if the choice is a familiar one. To fill your box, choose from this collection of birthday favorites:

Happy Birthday, Jesse Bear!
Written by Nancy White Carlstrom
Illustrated by Bruce Degen
Published by Simon & Schuster Children's Books

The Barn Party
Written & Illustrated by Nancy Tafuri
Published by Greenwillow Books

Don't Wake Up Mama! Another Five Little Monkeys Story
Written & Illustrated by Eileen Christelow
Published by Clarion Books

It's My Birthday
Written & Illustrated by Helen Oxenbury
Published by Candlewick Press

Sheep In A Shop
Written by Nancy Shaw
Illustrated by Margot Apple
Published by Houghton Mifflin Company

MONSTROUS EMOTIONS

Monsters are make-believe, right? Of course! But with some imagination, the monsters in this unit can really teach your little ones a lot about emotions. Ready? Boo! (Sorry, didn't mean to scare you.)

ideas contributed by dayle timmons

HAVE YOU EVER MET A MONSTER?

Well, what was it like? Ask your little ones to share with you what they imagine monsters are like. What makes a monster a certified monster, anyway? Where do monsters live? What do monsters eat? What do monsters do? Ever wonder what *monsters* are afraid of? Record youngsters' comments; then display their answers around the monster masterpieces described in the following activity.

Monsters are very big! Monsters look funny! Monsters eat everything! Monsters are awake at night. They're not afraid of the dark! Monsters act silly.

MONSTER MASTERPIECES

There's something monstrously creative afoot in this group activity. In advance enlarge the outline shapes of several monsters (see pages 18 and 19) onto bulletin-board paper. Divide your class into as many small groups as you prepared monster outlines. Gather each group of children around an outline and ask them what they think a truly magnificent monster would look like. Then provide the group with paint, scissors, glue, and assorted craft materials such as printed paper, shredded paper, crepe-paper streamers, and sequins. Encourage the children to use their creative efforts to bring the monster shape to life. When the projects are complete, cut out each group's monster; then display the monsters on a wall. There now—something you've created can't be all that scary, can it?

WE'RE GOING ON A MONSTER HUNT

Imaginary monsters seem to hide in the scariest places! Leading youngsters in the following chant will help them conquer their fears of sometimes scary places and even introduce them to a friendly monster!

We're going on a monster hunt.
We're going to find a big one!
We're not scared, but...

What if he's under the bed? Better go over it. Squoosh, squoosh, squoosh.
What if he's in the closet? Better close it. Slam, slam, slam.
What if he's behind the curtains? Better open them. Swish, swish, swish.
What if he's in the hallway? Better tiptoe down it. Tiptoe, tiptoe.
What if he's in the garage? Better stomp through it. Stomp, stomp, stomp.

Aahh! It's a monster!
What's that you said?
You're big, but you're friendly, and you want to go to bed?

Now we're not afraid of monsters, so...
Stomp through the garage,
Walk through the hallway,
Close the curtains,
Open the closet,
Jump into bed,
And turn out the lights! Click!

MONSTER MASKS

Here's a creative way for youngsters to learn that some things that scare us aren't what they seem to be. To make her own monster mask, a child embellishes a solid-colored paper plate with her choice of craft materials, such as cotton balls, buttons, pipe cleaners, curling ribbon, Styrofoam® pieces, muffin-pan liners, beans, audiotape from broken cassettes, and more. Tape a personalized craft stick onto the back of each child's mask. Then invite each child to hold her mask in front of her face as she is featured in the following song. The remainder of the group will have a frightfully fun time showing scared faces as the featured child makes her scariest sound.

SCARY MONSTERS
(sung to the tune of "Have You Ever Seen A Lassie?")

[Child's name] is a scary monster, scary
    monster, scary monster.
[Child's name] is a scary monster.
Let's hear [his/her] scary sound!

15

MONSTERS HAVE FEELINGS, TOO

If thoughts of monsters make children afraid, how do thoughts of children make monsters feel? Use this activity to suggest to your little ones that monsters have feelings, too. In advance enlarge one of each different monster on pages 18 and 19 onto a different color of construction paper. As you show each monster to your group, ask that students look closely at the monster's pose and facial expression to decide how it feels. Ask for reasons based on youngsters' own experiences to explain that monster's emotion. Then have children show similar expressions on their faces. Conclude the activity with a monster parade, marching past a mirror so that each child can review his favorite monster face.

FEELINGS, NOTHING MORE THAN FEELINGS

Woe, woe, woe, feelings. What do you do when you feel the way you do? Discuss natural and appropriate behaviors associated with various feelings. Follow up your discussion with the following rhyme and song. If desired, use the enlarged monsters from "Monsters Have Feelings, Too" as visual cues for each line or verse.

IF I WERE A MONSTER

If I were a happy monster, I'd go ha, ha, ha!
If I were a sad monster, I'd go boo, hoo, hoo.
If I were a mad monster, I'd go stomp, stomp, stomp!
If I were a scared monster, I'd go AAHH! AAHH! AAHH!
But I'm just me, you see, so I'll go [sound or action of child's choice].

MONSTER EMOTIONS
(sung to the tune of "If You're Happy And You Know It")

Happy monsters like to sing and clap their hands.	Clap hands.
Happy monsters like to sing and clap their hands.	Clap hands.
Happy monsters like to sing.	
Happy monsters clap their hands.	
Happy monsters like to sing and clap their hands.	Clap hands.
Sad monsters sometimes frown and start to cry…	Rub eyes.
Mad monsters stop to think, then count to five…	Count to five.
Scared monsters gulp and think of something nice…	Gulp.
Proud monsters stand up tall and say, "Hooray!"	Say, "Hooray!"

NO MONSTERS AT MY HOUSE!

Get ready for big language fun with this book that reviews the many emotions of monsters. Duplicate one of each different monster pattern on pages 18 and 19 onto different colors of construction paper. Cut out the monsters, corresponding colors of house shapes, and a white house shape. Program the pages with text as shown. On the white house, have each class member draw his picture. Laminate the monsters and houses. On the center of each colored house shape, attach the loop side of a Velcro® piece. On the back of each monster, attach the hook side of a Velcro® piece. Bind the pages together so that the illustrated white page is last. During a group time, give each monster to a child. As you chant the text and keep a steady beat for each page, have the child with the matching monster attach it to the page.

A mad monster lives in a red house, red house, red house.
A mad monster lives in a red house. That's where a mad monster lives.

Mad Monster

But no monsters live with me!

MONSTER MATCH

Parents are sure to appreciate the opportunity this take-home game provides for getting in touch with their little ones' feelings. For every child, duplicate each pair of matching monster cards (pages 18 and 19) onto a different color of paper. Cut out the cards; then place them in a resealable plastic bag along with a copy of the parent note on page 19. There's no make-believe here—each family's sure to have fun!

BEASTLY BOOKS

These delightful titles will reassure your little ones that they have the power to turn imaginary beasts into mild-mannered monsters.

The Monster At The End Of This Book
Written by Jon Stone & Illustrated by Mike Smollin
Published by Western Publishing Company, Inc.; 1995

Harry And The Terrible Whatzit
Written & Illustrated by Dick Gackenbach
Published by Houghton Mifflin Company, 1979

Go Away, Big Green Monster!
Written & Illustrated by Ed Emberley
Published by Little, Brown and Company; 1993

There's A Monster Under My Bed
Written by James Howe & Illustrated by David Rose
Published by Simon & Schuster Children's Books, 1986

Monster Patterns

Use with "Monster Masterpieces" on page 14, "Monsters Have Feelings, Too" and "Feelings, Nothing More Than Feelings" on page 16, and "No Monsters At My House!" and "Monster Match" on page 17.

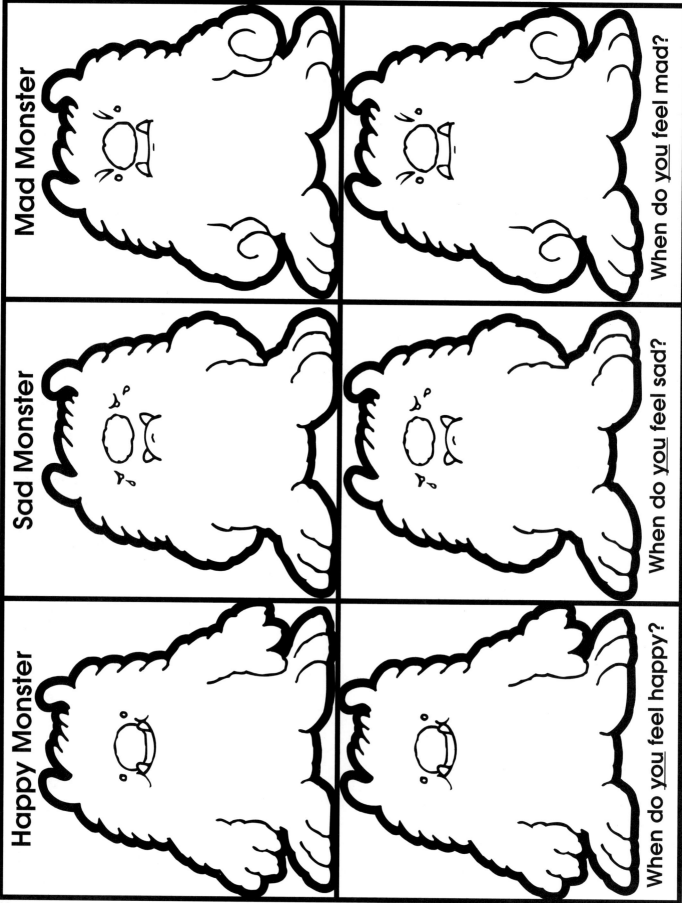

Mad Monster

When do you feel mad?

Sad Monster

When do you feel sad?

Happy Monster

When do you feel happy?

DEAR PARENT,

Get in touch with your "little monster's" feelings with this monster-match game. To play, display all of the monster cards. Ask your child to choose a card, then name that monster's emotion. Challenge your child to find the card with the matching monster. Then ask your child to tell you about a time when he/she felt that monster's emotion. Be sure to share your feelings, too! Have a monstrously fun time!

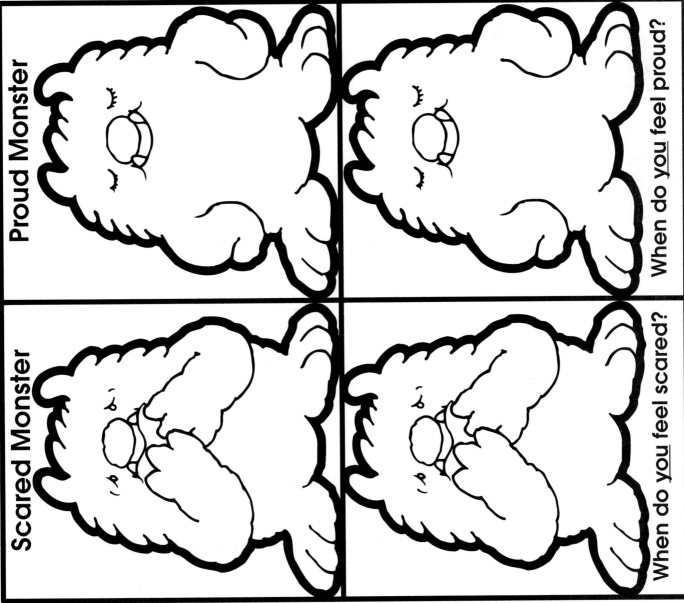

Proud Monster

When do you feel proud?

Scared Monster

When do you feel scared?

Pizza Pizzazz!

Looking for a hot topic your youngsters can really sink their teeth into? Bring out the checkered tablecloths and slice into this spicy topic during October, National Pizza Month. *ideas by Lucia Kemp Henry*

Accept No Substitutes

Since there are no substitutes for actual hands-on experiences, contact a local pizza parlor and ask if they conduct field trips for preschoolers. Explain that it would be good for youngsters to see pizzas being made and/or to have an opportunity to make a pizza. Follow up a pizza-parlor field trip by mailing a student-autographed, pizza-shaped note of thanks to your field-trip guides.

Come Into The Kitchen

What fun it must be to toss a crust into the air, slop the sauce onto the crust, and sprinkle on handfuls of toppings! Set up this pizzeria kitchen center, so that each youngster will have an opportunity to put himself in the role of a pizza chef. Stock the center with appropriate props, such as aprons, chef hats, and photo-illustrated pizza menus. At the kitchen center, place utensils usually associated with pizza-making, such as varying sizes of pizza pans and rolling pins. Cut several imitation pizza crusts and corresponding sauce circles from felt to fit your pans. Use the patterns from page 25 to trace and cut toppings from appropriate colors of felt, other fabrics, or wallpaper samples. Cut felt into short, narrow strips to resemble shredded cheese. Label a container for each topping and place the corresponding cutouts inside.

Once the center is operational, a student dons an apron, rolls out and tosses the crust for his pizza, spreads the sauce onto the crust, and sprinkles on the toppings of his choice. Photograph each chef with his culinary masterpiece, before asking the student to sort his toppings into their original containers. When each student has been photographed with his pizza, attach the photos to a bulletin board to resemble a giant menu (like the one at the right). Near each photo write a student-dictated description of the pictured pizza.

Luigi's Menu

Jacob's pizza sauce is made from a secret family recipe. The pepperoni is good too.

Pepperoni by Jacob

Jackie's pizza is made with a thin, crunchy crust. It's loaded with peppers, pepperoni, and pineapple.

Supreme by Jackie

Ryan says his pizza is the best. It has lots and lots and lots of cheese.

Cheese by Ryan

This pizza is spicy and hot because Sue likes it that way!

Pizza-Box Puzzles

To get your pizza theme off to a zesty start, make several construction-paper pizzas to fit inside small pizza boxes. Using construction-paper copies of the patterns on page 25, decorate each paper pizza with a different construction-paper topping, such as pepperoni, mushrooms, black olives, pineapple tidbits, cheese, or green peppers. Laminate each pizza and cut it into several pieces to make a puzzle; then place the pieces inside a pizza box. Divide your students into small groups and give each group one of these pizza boxes. Encourage each group of students to assemble its pizza puzzle. When each group has completed its puzzle, have the students tell what toppings are on their pizzas. Then discuss your youngsters' favorite toppings. Make a bar or pie graph, if desired, to indicate your youngsters' topping preferences.

Culinary Masterpieces To Go

Concocting a pizza is so much fun, you may want to give students more than one opportunity to try it. At the center described in "Come Into The Kitchen" on page 20, replace the felt cutouts with paper ones and provide glue. Also include scissors and additional paper so that students can create their own toppings if they wish. Then give each student an opportunity to create a culinary masterpiece that he can take home. Since take-out pizzas are best transported in boxes, provide a piece of folded bulletin-board paper to serve as a pizza box for each student. When a student's pizza is ready for transport, slip it inside the folded paper. As the student dictates, write something about his pizza on the outside of the folded paper. "Guess what? The pizza dude is here!"

Pizza-Pie Chant

Here's a rhythmic movement activity that's not only good enough to sink your teeth into; you can also sink your whole body into it. Write the "Pizza Chant" in large letters on chart paper. Embellish the margins with colorful pizza stickers or sketches of pizza toppings. As your youngsters chorally say the first verse of the "Pizza Chant," have them clap to the beat. Once youngsters have mastered the combination of chanting and clapping, have them march in place and later march in a circle as they chant.

As youngsters move to the beat of this chant, begin to vary the wording to heighten their interest. Modify the second verse of the chant to indicate each student's topping preference.

Pizza Chant

Piz-za, piz-za. Let's have piz-za!
Let's have piz-za with cheese on top!

Piz-za, piz-za. Let's have piz-za!
[Student's name] wants piz-za with [child's favorite topping] on top!

Strike Up The Band

Teach your youngsters the lyrics to this pizza tune. Then give each student an opportunity to take part in one of the world's most unusual bands. Provide youngsters with pizza-making utensils such as wooden spoons, pizza pans, rolling pins, measuring cups, and mixing bowls. Discuss with your youngsters the typical uses for the items. Encourage creative discussions about different ways that these utensils can be used to produce music. After giving the band an opportunity to warm up, have students sing "The Pizza Song" and accompany themselves with their highly unusual rhythm instruments. It's a "lotta" fun!

The Pizza Song
(sung to the tune of "Twinkle, Twinkle, Little Star")

Pizza, pizza. It's a treat.
Pizza pie is fun to eat!
Ooey-gooey cheese so yummy.
Crunchy crust goes in my tummy.
Pizza, pizza. It's a treat.
Pizza pie is fun to eat!

Poetic Pizza-Making

If you're going to make pizza from scratch, consider sharing this poem with your youngsters to introduce the basic steps of pizza-making.

Now We're Cookin'

Flour and water in a bowl.
Mix, mix, mix, and roll, roll, roll.
Roll the dough as flat as you can.
Put the dough in a pizza pan.
Spread the sauce; sprinkle with cheese.
Add some toppings, as you please.
Bake the pie until it's done.
Eat the pizza. Oh, what fun!
—*Lucia Kemp Henry*

Easy Minipizzas

If you're not quite up for making pizza from scratch, you'll love these quick-and-easy minipizzas. Encourage students to take turns grating mozzarella cheese and slicing some easy-to-slice pizza toppings. Have each student spoon a small amount of pizza sauce onto a bagel- or muffin-half and spread the sauce to the edges. Then have him add cheese and the toppings of his choice. Place several minipizzas on a baking sheet and broil them until the cheese melts. Cut each minipizza in half. When the pizzas are cool enough to eat, serve them to students. As students are enjoying their pizzas, discuss the meanings of half and whole.

Mouthwatering Matchup

Duplicate and cut out copies of the patterns on pages 24 and 25. Assemble pairs of pizza halves, so that each pair features a different topping. Glue the pieces in place. For each set of pizza halves, glue a cutout of the featured topping to the middle of a paper plate. Place the pizza halves and the paper plates inside a clean pizza box, and place the box in a center. To use the center, a student finds two halves to match the topping on each plate; then he puts the matching halves in each plate.

Seriously Silly

This student-made book gets sillier with every slice. Begin by cutting finger-paint paper into large circular shapes. Have each student finger-paint his circle to resemble sauce-covered dough. While these papers are drying, ask your youngsters to dictate a list of toppings that are found on real pizzas. Then ask them to think of things that could be put on make-believe pizzas. Provide a wide range of duplicate pictures cut from flower, garden, or seed catalogs. Have each child select multiple pictures of the same kind of object for a silly make-believe pizza; then have him attach the pictures to his finger-painted circle. Attach each student's pizza to a different sheet of art paper. As the student dictates, write something on the art paper about the pizza that he has created. Bind these student-prepared pages between covers, before titling the booklet and decorating the front cover appropriately.

Silly Pizza Pies

Jessica put flowers on a pizza!

Pam Crane

World's Best Pizza

Spirit your students away to the home of the world's best pizza. Read aloud Karen Barbour's Little Nino's Pizzeria (Harcourt Brace Jovanovich, Publishers). Discuss with the students what made Little Nino's Pizzeria and Little Tony's Pizzeria special. Talk in detail about what the world's best pizza would taste like. Discuss the crust, the sauce, the spices, and the toppings. Then ask each student to take a turn role-playing with you. Videotape the interviews if possible. Holding a microphone and playing the part of a television reporter, interview each child as though he has just come out of Little Nino's Pizzeria or Little Tony's Pizzeria. Introduce yourself and your network, and ask him to describe for your viewers what the world's best pizza tastes like. Lead the interviews so that each child has an opportunity to give a vivid description of the pizza to top all pizzas. Later send the video home for each child's parents in turn to enjoy; or invite parents to see a showing of the video before or after school.

Pizza-Half Patterns
Use with "Mouthwatering Matchup" on page 23.

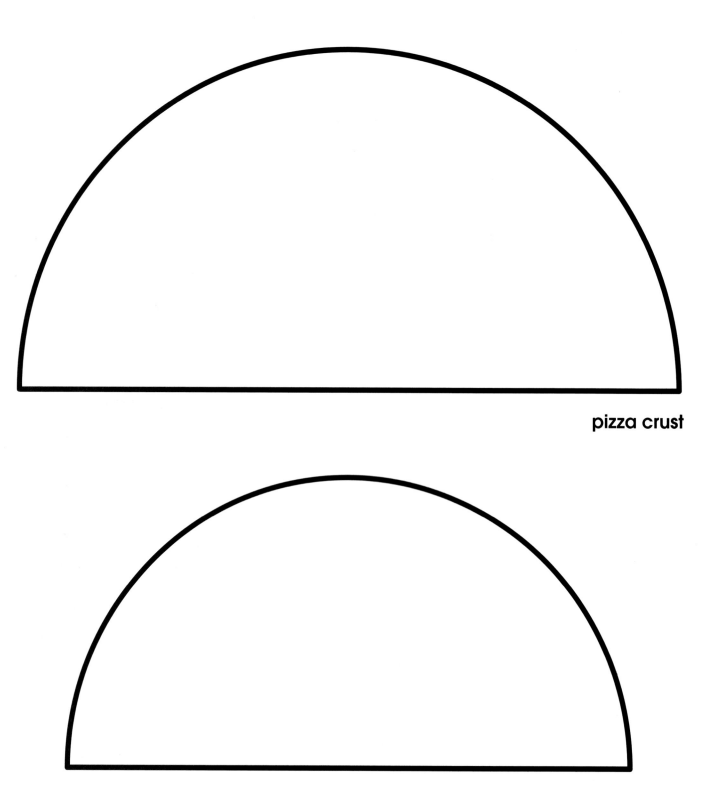

pizza crust

pizza sauce

Use with "Come Into The Kitchen" on page 20, "Culinary Masterpieces To Go" and "Pizza-Box Puzzles" on page 21, and "Mouthwatering Matchup" on page 23.

pepperoni

mushrooms

green pepper

olives

pineapple

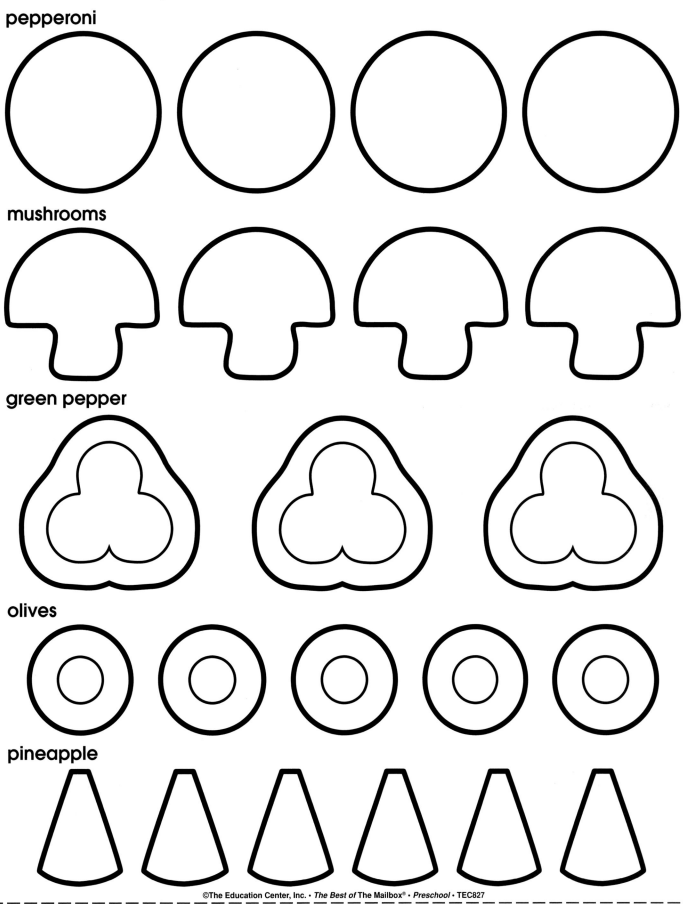

Note To Teacher: Cut small white paper or felt to resemble grated cheese.

Peanut Butter, Peanut Butter ....Jelly!

First you take the nuts and you crack 'em and you smash 'em. Then you take the grapes and you pick 'em and you squish 'em. Peanut butter and jelly—tasty treats for teeny tummies. Open up this unit and spread out the learning fun!

ideas by Carrie Lacher

"Peanutty" Chanting

Tickle youngsters' taste buds and tummies by reading aloud the popular chant *Peanut Butter And Jelly* as illustrated by Nadine Bernard Westcott (Puffin Books). Once youngsters are familiar with the rhyme, encourage active participation by providing each child with a peanut puppet. To make peanut puppets for each child and yourself, duplicate the peanut pattern on page 31 onto tan construction paper. Cut out the patterns; then glue each peanut to a separate craft stick. Write the letter *P* or the word *peanut* on each stick. Next write the chant on a large, bread-shaped piece of bulletin-board paper; then mount it at students' eye level. As the class chants the rhyme, use your peanut puppet to point to the words. Encourage youngsters to lift their puppets each time they recognize or say the word *peanut*. Get ready—your preschoolers are sure to go "peanutty"!

How *Do* They Do It?

How do spoonfuls of peanut butter and blobs of jelly wind up in a sandwich? If your little ones would like to know how peanuts turn into butter and grapes into jelly, then share with them the information and photographs in these excellent resources.

Make Me A Peanut Butter Sandwich And A Glass Of Milk
Written & Photographed by Ken Robbins
(Out of print. Check your library.)

My First Book Of How Things Are Made: Crayons, Jeans, Guitars, Peanut Butter, & More
Written & Photographed by George Jones
Published by Scholastic Inc.

From Peanuts To Peanut Butter
Written by Melvin Berger
Published by Newbridge Communications, Inc
(This big book can be ordered directly from Newbridge at 1-800-867-0307.)

Cooking Up Some PB 'n' J!

Mouthwatering measurement and following delicious directions are two of the tasty skills your little ones will learn when they participate in cooking up some real peanut butter and grape jelly. Since the grape jelly will need to congeal overnight, you might want to make the jelly one day and the peanut butter the next. Be sure to follow up your kitchen capers with the hands-on (or should we say *mouths-on*) math lesson described in "A Mouthful Of Math."

Groovy Grape-Juice Jelly

1 grape per child

2 cups bottled grape juice

one 3-fluid-ounce pouch of Certo® liquid fruit pectin

4 cups sugar

2 tablespoons water

To demonstrate how grape juice is made, give each child an opportunity to press a grape through a sieve. Then ask volunteers to help you measure the sugar and then the bottled grape juice into a large bowl. When each child has had a chance to stir the mixture, set it aside for about ten minutes. Combine the fruit pectin with the water in a small bowl; then pour the mixture into the juice-sugar mixture. Once again have each child stir the mixture, continuing until the sugar is no longer grainy. Pour the liquid into a container, seal it with a lid, and allow it to remain at room temperature overnight. The next day put the jelly in a refrigerator for up to three weeks. (For firmer jelly, store it in the refrigerator for several days before serving.)

Blissful Blender Peanut Butter

one 12-ounce package salted, roasted peanuts in the shell (or 1–2 cups shelled peanuts)

2 tablespoons vegetable oil

Invite youngsters to a table to help you shell peanuts. Pour the package of peanuts into several small bowls. Designate several empty bowls for the collection of the peanuts only. Encourage youngsters to shell the peanuts. (Keep trash cans nearby!) When the nuts are shelled, pour them into the blender. Add the vegetable oil; then blend the peanuts until smooth. (Use a spatula to scrape the peanut butter from the sides of the blender.) Store the peanut butter in a container in the refrigerator.

A Mouthful Of Math

With a tasty theme like peanut butter, eating the topic is half the fun! To make use of your class-made peanut butter and jelly *and* to introduce the concepts of half and whole, have your little ones make miniature sandwiches. Provide each child with a plastic knife, two slices of cocktail-sized bread, and a paper plate. Encourage each child to independently make a miniature peanut-butter-and-jelly sandwich. When you and each of your students have prepared a sandwich, introduce the word *whole*. Then cut your sandwich in *half* and place both halves atop a child's whole sandwich to demonstrate that two halves equal a whole. Have children cut their own sandwiches in half. Then have them sink their teeth into this early introduction to fractions!

Smoosh And Goosh

Your little ones won't be able to wait to get their hands on these nutty-tasting and sweet-smelling play doughs! Give youngsters plenty of opportunities to describe smells, textures, and colors as they sink their hands into each dough and smoosh and goosh their way into peanut-butter-and-jelly play. By the way, the peanut-butter dough is edible—so little ones with clean hands can be encouraged to eat their creations. The jelly dough smells mighty nice, but is just for hands-on fun.

Power-Packed Peanut-Butter Play Dough

2 cups creamy peanut butter
2 cups honey
4 1/2 cups powdered milk

Mix the honey and peanut butter together in a large bowl. Slowly add the powdered milk and knead the mixture until the dough is of a thick consistency. Store the dough in a sealed container and refrigerate when not in use.

Jammin' Jelly Play Dough

5 tablespoons cream of tartar
3/4 cup salt
3 cups all-purpose flour
.14-ounce package of unsweetened, grape-flavored drink mix
3 cups water
3 tablespoons vegetable oil
blue and red food coloring

Stir all of the dry ingredients into a large pot. Slowly add the water and oil. Using a large wire whisk, blend the mixture until all of the lumps are gone. Whisk in several drops of blue and red food coloring until the mixture is a medium purple color. (The dough will darken as it cooks.) Cook the mixture over medium heat, stirring constantly with a large spoon until it forms a ball. While the mixture is still warm, knead it on a lightly floured board for several minutes or until the dough has a soft, satiny feel. Store the dough in a sealed container at room temperature for up to a month.

Start Spreading The News!

The smell of these sandwich collages is here to stay! Little ones will get a real feel for sandwich making with this scented, sticky-fingered art exploration. For each child, cut pairs of bread, peanut butter, and jelly shapes (patterns on page 31) from white, brown, and purple tissue paper. To make a collage, remove the backing from a length of clear Con-Tact® covering. Tape the covering to a table with the sticky side up. Have a child arrange and press his pieces onto the covering. Give him purple glitter and a small amount of a powdered, grape-flavored drink mix to sprinkle over the covering. When the child is satisfied with his project, press on a length of plastic wrap. Trim the edges; then display the sandwich collage on a window. Ahh—the sights and smells of a peanut-butter-and-jelly sandwich!

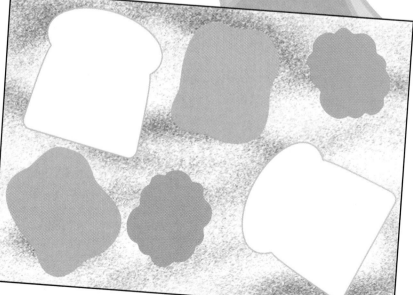

What's For Lunch?

Tempt youngsters to visit this math center by filling lunchboxes with sandwiches made for counting. Using the patterns on page 31, duplicate ten pairs of the bread shape onto white paper, ten peanut-butter shapes onto tan paper, and ten jelly shapes onto purple paper. Label each of the peanut-butter shapes, each of the jelly shapes, and each pair of bread shapes with a different numeral and dot set from one to ten. Laminate the shapes for durability before cutting them out. Place the sandwich fixings in lunchboxes along with ten resealable plastic bags. When visiting the center, a child makes sandwiches by finding the bread slices, peanut butter, and jelly that have corresponding numerals and dot sets. He then places each sandwich set in a plastic bag. Lunchtime!

A Sticky Song

Your little ones are sure to get stuck on this sweet sandwich song!

Peanut Butter 'n' Jelly
(sung to the tune of "Shortnin' Bread")

Chorus:
Peanut butter 'n' jelly,
Jelly, jelly,
Peanut butter 'n' jelly,
Mmm-mmm good.

Verses:
Peanut butter's chewy.
Jelly's nice and sweet.
Put them both together—
Mmm! What a treat!

Fixing up a sandwich.
Gonna make it right.
Get ready, mouth
For a great big bite!

Repeat chorus, singing as if your mouth is full of a great big bite!

Disappearing Sandwiches!

Here's a peanut of a tale that will have youngsters eating out of the palm of your hand. In advance prepare five felt sandwiches to accompany the flannelboard rhyme below. Using the bread pattern on page 31, cut five bread shapes from white felt. Hot-glue each bread shape to a slightly larger piece of purple felt; then cut around the shape. Hot-glue each pair of bread-and-jelly pieces to slightly larger pieces of brown felt; then cut around the shape. Add finishing touches to each sandwich using markers or fabric paint. During a group time, display all five sandwich look-alikes on a flannelboard. As you recite each verse of the rhyme, name a different volunteer to remove a sandwich from the board.

Five Tasty Sandwiches

Five tasty sandwiches of jelly and peanut butter,
[Child's name] took one to share with his brother.

Four tasty sandwiches as chewy as can be,
[Child's name] took one—now there are three.

Three tasty sandwiches, I made them just for you.
[Child's name] took one—now there are two.

Two tasty sandwiches with jelly nice and sweet,
[Child's name] took one for an after-school treat.

How many sandwiches? Uh oh, there's just one.
[Child's name]'s taking it—now there are none.

Peanut-Butter-And-Jelly Jiggling

These simple, gross-motor games are sure to have all of your little nuts jumping and jiggling for joy.

Peanut Butter, Peanut Butter...Jelly!

Your little ones will quickly catch on to this thematic version of Duck, Duck, Goose. Seat your students in a circle on the floor. To play, a volunteer leader walks around the outside of the circle while lightly tapping each seated child on the head and saying "Peanut butter." When desired, the leader taps a child and announces, "Jelly!" At that cue, the tapped child jumps up and chases the leader around the circle. The leader runs to sit in an open spot in the circle or the tapped child catches him and they both stop. Either way, the tapped child now becomes the leader. Play continues until each child has a turn as the leader.

Peanut-Butter-And-Jelly Roll

Seat youngsters in a circle on the floor. Give one child a purple ball to represent a giant grape. To play, the group chants, "Peanut butter, peanut butter, peanut butter, JELLY!" On the word "JELLY!" the child holding the ball names another child in the circle and rolls the ball to that child. As a variation, ask older children to pass the ball around the circle while chanting. Continue play until each child has rolled the ball.

The jelly slipped out of my sandwich.

Nathan

That's A Big Sandwich!

A unit as delightfully filling as this one demands an extrabig finish. Capture all the tasty fun by asking students to help you fill a sandwich big book with their favorite peanut-butter-and-jelly memories. In advance enlarge the bread pattern on page 31; then cut a classroom supply of bread shapes from 12" x 18" sheets of white construction paper. Write on each child's bread shape as he dictates his favorite peanut-butter experience; then have him illustrate his page. To prepare covers for your sandwich big book, use the enlarged pattern to trace a bread shape onto two thin pieces of foam. Cut out the shapes; then add details using fabric paint. Bind the pages between the foam covers using large metal rings. Your little ones will enjoy hearing you read about their experiences, and afterward the giant book will make a wonderfully tasteful addition to your classroom library.

Use with " 'Peanutty' Chanting" on page 26; "Start Spreading The News!" on page 28; "What's For Lunch?"
and "Disappearing Sandwiches!" on page 29; and "That's A Big Sandwich!" on page 30.

bread

peanut

peanut butter

jelly

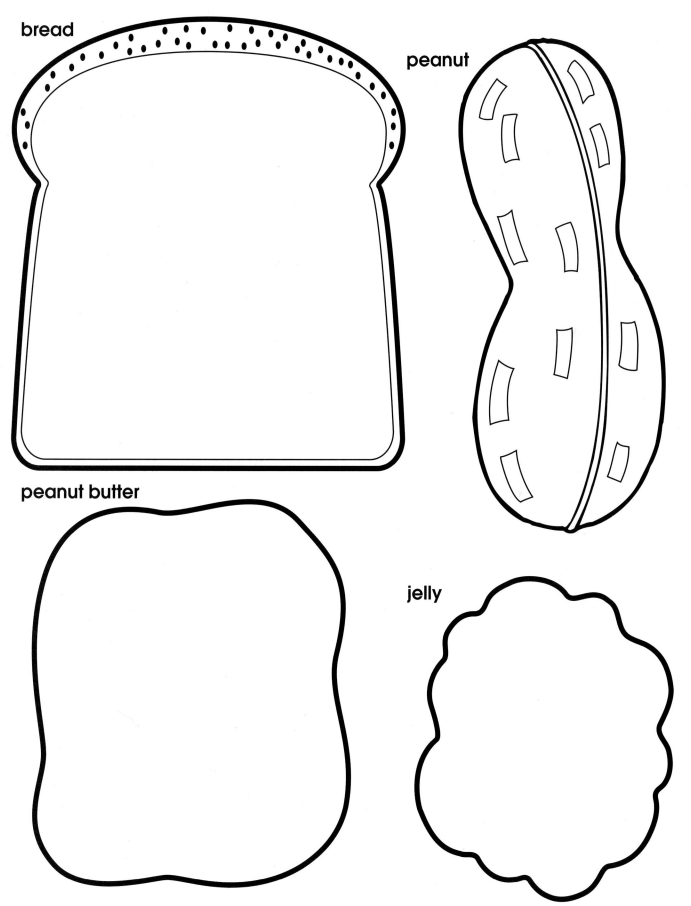

Celebrate In Centers

Celebrate the diversity of our valued traditions with these seasonal centers.

ideas contributed by Linda Blassingame and Lori Kent

Seasonal Center Setup

To fill your classroom with holiday merriment and learning fun, set up the centers described on pages 33–36. Then use this system to indicate which of the centers relate to Hanukkah, Christmas, or Kwanzaa. Reproduce the blank candle pattern (page 37) onto blue paper for each Hanukkah center, red for each Christmas center, and green for each Kwanzaa center. Cut out the candles; then display the appropriate color of candle in each center. What a room full of diverse learning opportunities!

Tyler

Dear Parent,

Happy Holidays!

Play-Dough Center

Menorah Mats

Cooking Center

Kwanzaa Kabobs

Music Center

Bell Exploration

Paint Center

Kwanzaa Flags

Tactile Center

Santa's Beard

Candle Collections

This management system is a bright way to record the centers each child visits, and spark parents' interest in your classroom activities as well! For each child, duplicate a copy of the parent note and booklist (page 37) onto white construction paper. Personalize the parent-note candles; then cut all the candles out. For each center, program a blank candle with that center's name and activity. Then duplicate a class supply of that candle onto the appropriate color of construction paper so that it matches the candle displayed in the center. Cut out the candles; then store each set in its corresponding center.

To use this system, direct a child to take a candle cutout from each center he visits. Tape the candles to his parent note as shown, accordion-folding them to create a booklet. When he has visited the desired number of centers, tape the booklist to the last candle in his collection. Your little ones will shine with pride when they take these candle collections home to share with their families.

Hanukkah

These centers focus on the Jewish holiday Hanukkah—the Festival of Lights.

Dramatic-Play Center

Lots Of Latkes

Your little ones can cook up lots of Hanukkah latkes when you stock your dramatic-play area with a few frying pans, bowls, spoons, spatulas, an empty container of oil, and some aprons. Cut out brown construction-paper circles to resemble latkes; then laminate them. Encourage your youngsters to make pretend latkes while playing in this center.

Play-Dough Center

Menorah Mats

This play-dough center will have your little ones rolling with delight! Reproduce the menorah pattern (page 38) onto construction paper several times. Laminate each page; then place the mats in your play-dough center. Invite a child to roll play dough into candle shapes, then arrange them on a menorah mat. Challenge the child to count the number of play-dough candles on the menorah.

Cooking Center

Menorahs To Munch

Youngsters will get a tasty Hanukkah treat after making these munchable menorahs. Stock your cooking center with marshmallows, pretzel sticks, and resealable sandwich bags. Invite a child to make an edible menorah by counting out nine marshmallows onto a napkin, then pressing a pretzel into each one. Have him line up the marshmallows side by side to resemble a menorah. Encourage him to eat a few of the marshmallow and pretzel pieces. Direct him to place the remaining pieces in a resealable bag to take home and eat later.

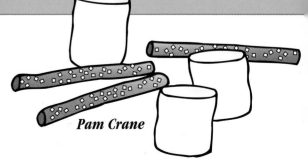

Pam Crane

Your little elves will have a "ho, ho, ho" lot of fun celebrating Christmas in these jolly centers!

Woodworking Center

Santa's Workshop

Turn your woodworking center into Santa's workshop with the addition of Styrofoam® pieces, empty spools, craft sticks, glue, and markers. Provide toy catalogs to help your busy workers gather ideas. Encourage a child visiting this center to make a toy for Santa's sleigh using the materials provided. To add a little touch of elfin delight, provide students with felt Santa hats to wear while they are hard at work.

Tactile Center

Santa's Beard Is Soft And White

Your little merrymakers will get a real feel for Santa's beard when visiting this tactile center. Enlarge the Santa pattern (page 39) onto a large sheet of white paper. Color the pattern. Tape it onto a tabletop; then cover it with clear Con-Tact® covering. Squirt a dollop of nonmenthol-scented shaving cream onto Santa's beard. Invite a child to use her fingers to give Santa a beard that is fluffy and white.

Gross-Motor Center

Holiday Beanbag Toss

Use this idea to toss some gross-motor fun into your holiday centers. Use an X-acto® knife to cut a Christmas-tree shape out of a piece of green foam board. Cut circles from the tree to resemble ornaments. Hot-glue the tree shape to a cylindrical container filled with sand. Place the tree on the floor in an open area. Place several beanbags in a gift-wrapped box near the tree. Invite one child in a pair to toss a beanbag through a hole in the tree. Have his partner stand near the tree, righting it if it falls. When all the beanbags have been tossed, have the pair return them to the box. Then direct the pair to change roles.

Shelly Dohogne—Early Childhood Special Education
Scott County Central, Sikeston, MO

Invite your little angels to celebrate the Advent season in these centers.

Away In The Manger

Youngsters will have lots of opportunities to build on their understanding of the first Christmas when you stock your block area with the figures from a nativity set, some straw, and fabric scraps. Encourage children to work in small groups to create a nativity scene using the materials provided.

Sensory Table

Angels All Around

Your little cherubs will enjoy this heavenly sorting experience. Fill your sensory table with Styrofoam® packing pieces and a quantity of cotton balls. Cut angel shapes from each of three different colors of construction paper. Laminate the angel shapes; then hide them in your sensory table. Make sorting pockets by cutting three cloud shapes from construction paper in corresponding colors to the angels; then glue each one onto a separate white paper bag. Tape the bags to the edge of your sensory table. Challenge a child visiting this center to find the angels, then sort them by color into the cloud pockets.

Music Center

Hear The Bells

The ringing of bells is a universal signal to call people together, announce news, and celebrate important events. Stock your music center with a wide variety of bells and some recorded Christmas music featuring bells. Invite a child to explore the sound of each bell, then shake his choice of bells as he listens to the recorded music. Now that's some jolly jingling!

35

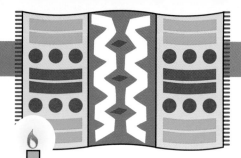

Kwanzaa

At these centers students can celebrate the values and traditions of African-Americans.

Paint Center

Kwanzaa Flags

Your little ones will learn the colors of Kwanzaa when making *benderas,* or flags. Stock your easel with large sheets of white construction paper and red, green, and black paint. Encourage a child to paint a flag as shown. When the paint is dry, tape his flag to a paint-stirring stick for a handle. When each child's flag is complete, lead students in a parade around the classroom as you play some traditional African music. Happy Kwanzaa!

Cooking Center

Kwanzaa Kabobs

Students will love preparing these delicious fruit kabobs to remind them of the bountiful harvest celebrated during Kwanzaa. In your cooking center, place a variety of fruit pieces such as pineapple, apples, bananas, oranges, and maraschino cherries. Add black paper plates and a supply of red and green toothpicks. Invite a small group of children to visit the center. Direct each child to skewer her choice of fruits onto red and green toothpicks to make kabobs. Then have her place her kabobs on a plate. When each child has prepared her kabobs, invite the group to sit together to celebrate the harvest.

Manipulative Center

African Trading Beads

To prepare this center, dye quantities of penne pasta red and green. Mix several drops of red or green food coloring with enough rubbing alcohol to soak the amount of pasta you would like to dye that color. Soak the pasta; then drain it before spreading it out to dry. Place the dry pasta and lengths of black yarn in a center. Encourage a child to string the pasta onto the yarn; then knot the ends together to form a necklace.

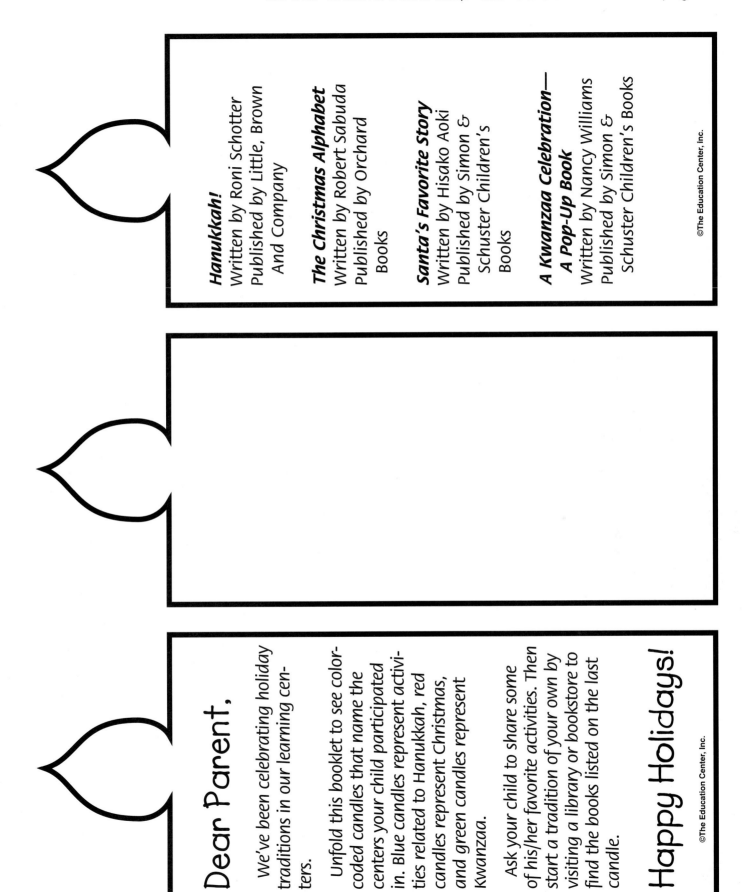

Hanukkah!
Written by Roni Schotter
Published by Little, Brown
And Company

The Christmas Alphabet
Written by Robert Sabuda
Published by Orchard
Books

Santa's Favorite Story
Written by Hisako Aoki
Published by Simon &
Schuster Children's
Books

**A Kwanzaa Celebration—
A Pop-Up Book**
Written by Nancy Williams
Published by Simon &
Schuster Children's Books

©The Education Center, Inc.

Dear Parent,

We've been celebrating holiday traditions in our learning centers.

Unfold this booklet to see color-coded candles that name the centers your child participated in. Blue candles represent activities related to Hanukkah, red candles represent Christmas, and green candles represent Kwanzaa.

Ask your child to share some of his/her favorite activities. Then start a tradition of your own by visiting a library or bookstore to find the books listed on the last candle.

Happy Holidays!

©The Education Center, Inc.

Menorah Pattern

Use with "Menorah Mats" on page 33.

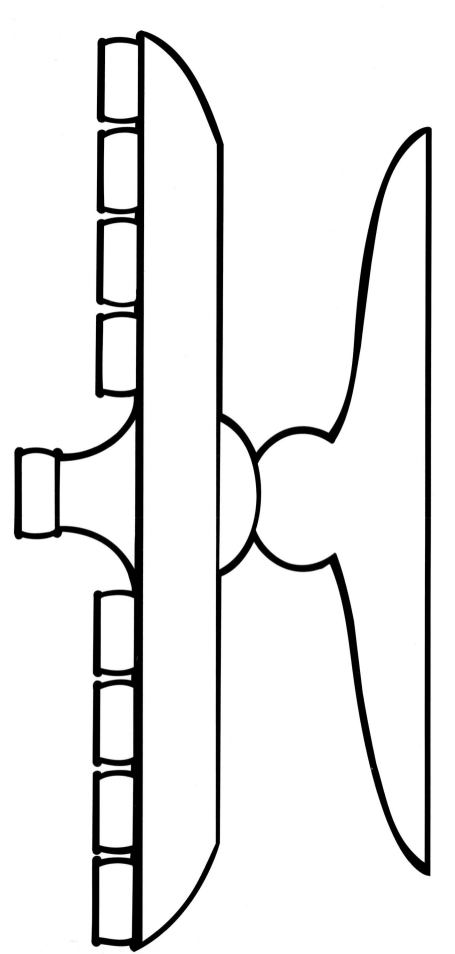

Santa Pattern

Use with "Santa's Beard Is Soft And White" on page 34.

A Cookie For You And A Cookie For Me

Who should take the cookies from the cookie jar? You should take the cookies from the cookie jar— and share them with your class! Find out how sweet sharing can be when you practice with cookies!

ideas contributed by Henry Fergus

Ding, Dong!

Did someone hear the doorbell ring? Introduce your sharing theme with the crowd-pleasing *The Doorbell Rang* by Pat Hutchins (Greenwillow Books). Bring a class supply of chocolate-chip cookies (plus a few extra) to your group area; then begin munching on a cookie or two in front of your class. When your children have figured out that you're up to something, state with surprise that you forgot to share! Then give each child a cookie to munch on while you read the story aloud. Pause to ask what the children in the story should do when all of the cookies have been shared and the doorbell rings *again*. Then share the surprise ending. More cookies, anyone?

One For You, And One For You, And One For You...

This activity will make your snacktime extrasweet and continue to teach the goodness of sharing. Put as many cookies in a jar as you have seats at a table. Ring a bell each time you invite a child to sit down and take a cookie from the jar. When the seats are filled and the cookies have been shared, invite everyone to eat. Vary the activity by substituting cookies with other single-serving items, such as crackers or flavored mini rice cakes. There's enough for everyone!

Let's Share

Sing this song during your snacktime or anytime you need to encourage sharing.

Share With Me
(sung to the tune of "This Old Man")

One for you; one for me.
Let's all sing this melody.
Come and share with me and I will share with you.
Sharing is so fun to do!

Who Shared The Cookie From The Cookie Jar?

Reinforce sharing with this tasty circle-time game based on a popular chant. Cut out a class supply of paper cookies; then label each one with a different child's name. Put the cookies in a cookie jar. During a group time, ask a volunteer to take a cookie from the jar; then identify the child's name on the cookie. Have the class join you in reciting the following chant, substituting the volunteer's name and the name on the cookie. Then have the volunteer give the cookie to the appropriate child. Invite that child to be the next person to take a cookie from the jar. Continue until each child has a cookie. To make the game even more fun, have each child give a real cookie to the child whose labeled cookie was selected.

Who shared a cookie from the cookie jar?
[Child's name] shared a cookie from the cookie jar.
[She/he] did? Yes, [she/he] did!
With whom?
With [name on cookie].

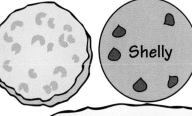

Shelly

A Cookie For You And A Cookie For Me

Your little ones are sure to internalize the joy of sharing when they give away cookies they've decorated themselves. To prepare, duplicate a class supply of both labels on page 43; then cut them apart. Write each child's name on a separate pair of labels; then add a different child's name to each of the "A Cookie For You" labels. Tape each label to a separate resealable plastic bag. Set up a cookie-decorating center with two cookies for each child, different colors of frosting, plastic knives, a variety of candy decorations, and napkins. Invite each child to visit the center to use her choice of items to decorate two cookies. As she puts one cookie in each of her two bags, explain that she will keep one of her cookies and share the other one. She will also get a cookie from a friend. When everyone has decorated cookies, give them to the students with great ceremony; then direct them to take their bags home. Sharing is delicious!

A Cookie For
You!
This sweet treat was made by
Karen
for
Scott

A Cookie For
Me!
Karen

Pretend Cookies; Real Sharing

Cook up some real sharing in your dramatic-play area by supplying just one of each different item needed to bake delicious imaginary cookies. Stock the center with a batch of cookie dough (play dough), one bowl, one spoon, one rolling pin, one cookie cutter, and one pan. Remind the children that in order to bake up a lot of cookies, they'll need to share the items. Sharing means more fun for everyone!

Please Share. Thank You!

Put social skills into practice with this tasty counting activity. For each child, duplicate the cookie-jar pattern on page 43 onto construction paper; then personalize it. Cut out the patterns. Working with a pair of children, give each child her jar and the same number of Cookie-Crisp® cereal pieces. To play, a child asks her partner for a number of cookies by saying, "May I please have [number] cookie(s)?" The second child then counts out that number of cookies from her jar and puts them onto her partner's jar. The first child says, "Thank you for sharing." The second child responds, "You're welcome." The second child then takes a turn. Continue until each child has had several turns; then provide each child with an individual bag of cereal pieces for snacking. Use the cookie jars with the incentive idea described in "Sharing Is So Sweet."

Sue

Sue shared the blocks at center time.

Sue

Sharing Is So Sweet

Use this display idea to share the good news of youngsters' social successes. When you observe a child sharing, record the circumstances on a paper cookie cutout. Glue the cookie to that child's jar. When each child's jar has one cookie, mount the jars on a display labeled "Sharing Is So Sweet!"

Celebrate Sharing

Celebrate your youngsters' success at sharing with a giant cookie. Follow the package directions on one or more refrigerated ready-to-bake pan cookies. When the cookie has cooled, divide it into pieces so that you have enough for each child and some extras to share with school staff or another class. *C* is for cookie. *C* is for celebration!

42

Sheila Krill

A Cookie For You!

This sweet treat was made by

_____

for

_____

A Cookie For Me!

_____

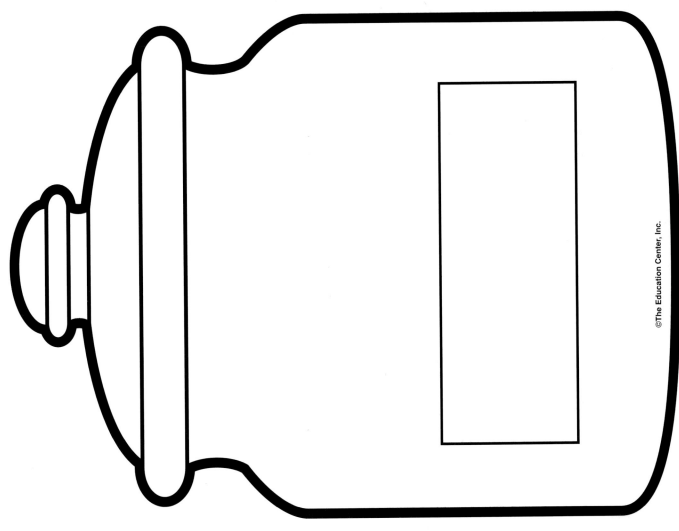

©The Education Center, Inc.

Pitter-Patter, Drip-Drop, Splish-Splash...Rain!

The forecast for this unit calls for showers of learning with frequent downpours of fun. Just pop open your umbrella and check out this flood of group-time and center-time activities.

Under The Weather

Create a storm of excitement when you use this idea to introduce youngsters to your rain theme. Prior to a group time, collect one umbrella for every two or three children. (Cover the umbrellas' tips with tape for safety.) Cover the floor of your group area with a plastic painting tarp or a plastic tablecloth. Put a bucket of water, a sponge, a raincoat, and the umbrellas near your chair. If desired, put an audiotape of rain sounds in a tape player that is also near your chair.

Begin the fun by putting on the raincoat, dimming your lights, and announcing that the weather forecast predicts rain. As the students take a seat on the plastic, give every two or three children an open umbrella to share. Turn on the audiotape; then quickly announce, "It's starting to rain!" Squeeze the water-filled sponge onto the umbrellas. Pitter-patter, hear the showers of laughter?

Henry Fergus—Preschool
Desert View Elementary
Phoenix, AZ

Reading In The Rain

After your surprise shower, wipe up the puddles and share any of these rainy-day stories that are just right for your preschool listeners.

Rain
Written by Robert Kalan
Illustrated by Donald Crews
Published by William Morrow And Company, Inc.

Wet World
Written by Norma Simon
Illustrated by Alexi Natchev
Published by Candlewick Press

In The Rain With Baby Duck
Written by Amy Hest
Illustrated by Jill Barton
Published by Candlewick Press

Listen To The Rain
Written by Bill Martin, Jr., and John Archambault
Illustrated by James Endicott
Published by Henry Holt And Company, Inc.

Noah's Ark
Written & Illustrated by Lucy Cousins
Published by Candlewick Press

Cloudy With A Choice Of Centers

You'll have clear skies ahead when you use this system to help youngsters make learning center choices. To prepare, cut a posterboard cloud shape for each rain-themed center you set up in your classroom. (See pages 45–47 for center suggestions.) Label each cloud with a different center's name. To each cloud, attach the hook side of as many Velcro® pieces as you will allow children in that center at one time. Put each cloud in its corresponding center. From laminated construction paper, cut a raindrop shape for each child. Personalize each drop; then attach the loop side of a piece of Velcro® to the back of it. Store the raindrops in a bucket.

When it is time for your children to choose centers, toss the raindrops in the air so that they rain down over your group. Announce each child's name as you pick up his raindrop. Then direct that child to attach his drop to the cloud in the center of his choice.

Henry Fergus, Phoenix, AZ

Dramatic Play

Drip-Drop Dramatic Play

Grab your galoshes and get ready for a rain-stompin', puddle-hoppin' good time at this dramatic-play center. Fill a wading pool with water-soluble packing pieces. Above the area, hang crepe-paper or metallic streamers to represent rain. Near the center, place a box filled with rain gear, such as galoshes, raincoats, and umbrellas. To really give the area a rainy-day feel, play an audiotape of rain sounds. If desired, fill a bucket with the books listed on page 44 so that properly attired youngsters can settle in for some wet and wild reading.

Carla Arnouville, Bordelonville, LA

Math Center

Just A Drop In The Bucket

Prepare this partner game for your math center, and soon it will be raining and pouring counting skills! Spray-paint both sides of 30 dried lima beans (plus some extra) blue. Divide the amount of beans in half; then store the halves in separate resealable plastic bags. Prepare a spinner, similar to the one shown, that displays numerals and matching numbers of raindrops. (To match your students' abilities, increase or decrease the number of divisions and the numerals on the spinner.) Also put two cups in the center to represent buckets.

To play, each child in a pair receives a bucket and bag of raindrops. In turn, each child spins the spinner, and then counts a matching number of raindrops into her bucket. The winner is the first child to count all 15 raindrops into her bucket.

Ellen Van De Walle—Preschool Consultant
Hendersonville Childcare Resource and Referral, Hendersonville, NC

Shower Power

The fun will go from a drizzle to a downpour at your water table when you add rainmaking items, such as colanders, strainers, sieves, watering cans, and sifters. If desired, invite visitors to this center to don raincoats and galoshes before reaching in to make it rain. And since the wet fun could get wild, keep some towels on hand as well.

Henry Fergus—Preschool, Desert View Elementary, Phoenix, AZ

Movement Area

Raindrops Keep Falling

Invite youngsters over to this movement center to do a rain dance, hop, skip, or jump! To prepare stuffed raindrops, fill five or more thin, blue children's socks with cotton balls; then knot the socks closed. On a length of blue bulletin-board paper, draw the outlines of five puddle shapes. Write a different numeral from 1 to 5 in each puddle. To use this center, a child tosses a raindrop into a puddle. He announces the numeral on that puddle; then he and his classmates at the center jump, hop, or clap the corresponding number of times. As a variation, draw ten puddles on the paper. Or challenge a child to throw the raindrops into the puddles in sequential order.

Ellen Van De Walle—Preschool Consultant
Hendersonville Childcare Resource and Referral, Hendersonville, NC

Sensory Center

April Showers Bring...Mud!

Invite youngsters to muddle around with these no-mess mud alternatives at your sensory center. Squirt brown liquid paint into several different sizes of sealable plastic bags. Seal the bags; then secure the seals with clear packing tape. Invite youngsters to use their fingers to create designs, shapes, or letters in the mud.

As another mud alternative, provide youngsters with this mushy mud dough for molding, mashing, and making mud pies. To make the mud dough, mix together 1/2 cup of cold water, one tablespoon of cooking oil, and two tablespoons of brown, washable liquid paint. Stir in 1/2 cup of salt; then add one tablespoon of cornstarch. Gradually add 1 1/2 cups of flour until the dough is soft and smooth. Store the dough in a container; then place it in a center along with plastic spatulas, plastic knives, and different sizes of aluminum tins. (If the dough gets sticky, add flour.) More mud, anyone?

Henry Fergus

Rainy-Day Blues, Reds, And Yellows

Add a splash of color to your rain unit with these umbrellas. To prepare this art center, cover a work surface with newspapers. Fill three small containers with water; then tint each container of water with a generous amount of either red, blue, or yellow food coloring. Place an eyedropper in each container. To make one project, provide a child with one good-quality white paper towel. Direct the child to drop the tinted water onto the paper towel until it is completely covered with color. When the towel is dry, cut out an umbrella shape. Have the child cut out a paper umbrella handle to glue to a large piece of construction paper. Then have him glue his umbrella onto the paper, over the handle. Let it rain!

Geri Covins, Rochester, MI

Rain Makes Rainbows!

Sunny smiles will pour out of your art center when your children create these magical rainbows of color. Cover a work surface with newspapers. For each child, cut a rainbow shape from a good quality white paper towel. Invite a child at the center to use water-based markers to draw wide stripes of different colors on one of the cutouts, leaving space between the stripes. Next have her use a paintbrush to apply water across the stripes. As the towel absorbs the water, the colors blend to create a beautiful rainbow!

Ellen Van De Walle—Preschool Consultant
Hendersonville Childcare Resource and Referral, Hendersonville, NC

Plop, Plop, Fizz, Fizz

After your weather watchers have visited your classroom rain centers, they're sure to enjoy Raindrop Fizzes from your cooking area. In advance, freeze ice cubes from water that has been tinted blue. (Freeze several ice cubes per child.) To make one drink, half-fill a plastic cup with a clear carbonated drink. Then drop several raindrops (ice cubes) into the drink. Plop, plop, fizz, fizz. Oh, what a fun drink this is!

Henry Fergus, Phoenix, AZ

Mud-Puddle Cookies

Invite your little ones to help make these "mud-licious" mud-puddle cookies to enjoy with their Raindrop Fizzes. To prepare the mud batter, beat one egg; then mix it into 2 1/2 cups of softened non-dairy topping. Fold in one package of devil's food moist cake mix (18.25 ounces). In a separate bowl, prepare the dirt mixture by combining 1/2 cup of confectioners' sugar with 1/2 cup cocoa. Plop a spoonful of the mud dough into the dirt mixture; then put the covered dough ball onto a greased cookie sheet. Bake at 350° for ten minutes. These mud puddles are mouthwateringly delicious!

adapted from an idea by Kimberli Carrier—Preschool, Wise Owl Preschool
Nashua, NH

Umbrella, Umbrella, Raindrops!

Save this version of the popular game Duck, Duck, Goose for a rainy day. Prior to playing, use a paper cutter to quickly prepare a supply of blue paper confetti to represent rain. To play, seat the class in a circle on the floor. Give a volunteer leader a small amount of the rain to hold in one hand. Direct the leader to walk around the outside of the circle while lightly tapping each seated child on the head and saying, "Umbrella." When desired, the leader drops the handful of rain over a child's head and announces, "Raindrops!" At that cue, the tapped child jumps up and chases the leader around the circle. The leader runs to sit in the open spot in the circle or the tapped child catches him and they both stop. Either way, the tapped child now becomes the leader. Play continues until each child has had a turn as the leader.

Kimberli Carrier—Preschool, Wise Owl Preschool, Nashua, NH

Let's Make Mud

Your class is sure to have a thunderous time with this mud-making activity! Prior to this group project, pour a small box of instant chocolate pudding into a clear bowl. Use blue food coloring to tint two cups of milk blue; then pour the milk into a sanitized watering can. Tape a white cloud cutout to the can. Collect enough flashlights and small plastic containers for each child to have one. To begin, give each child either a flashlight or a tub. Let the rainstorm begin by having the children turn their flashlights on and off to represent lightning, or tap their containers to represent thunder. Pour the rain (milk) over the dirt (pudding). Stir until the mud is smooth. When the storm is over, direct each child to wash his hands; then put a dollop of mud on a piece of waxed paper for each child. How delighted your little ones will be when they find out that the mud tastes good, too!

Carla Arnouville, Bordelonville, LA

Pam Crane

Balancing Raindrops

No one will take a rain check on the chance to participate in this movement activity! In advance, prepare a class supply of stuffed raindrops by filling thin, blue children's socks with cotton balls; then knot the socks closed (see "Raindrops Keep Falling" on page 46). Give each child a raindrop. As you sing the following song, challenge students to balance the raindrops on the named body part. Repeat the song, substituting a different body part each time.

(sung to the tune of "Frère Jacques")
Rain is falling, rain is falling,
On my [head], on my [head].
I can feel the raindrop, I can feel the raindrop,
On my [head], on my [head].

Ellen Van De Walle—Preschool Consultant
Hendersonville Childcare Resource and Referral, Hendersonville, NC

Singing In The Rain

Keep youngsters singing the rainy-day blues to these familiar tunes.

I've Been Listening To The Rain Fall

(sung to the tune of "I've Been Working On The Railroad")

I've been listening to the rain fall,
All the morning long.
I've been listening to the rain fall,
As I sing this little song.
Can't you hear the wind a-blowing,
Rustling through the trees?
Can't you hear the thunder rumbling?
Now sing this song with me.

Come out, Mr. Sun. Come out, Mr. Sun.
Come out, Mr. Sun, today and stay!
Come out, Mr. Sun. Come out, Mr. Sun.
So we can go out and play!

Melissa Pyles—Headstart
Carter St. Headstart of Childhood Development Services
Inverness, FL

Waiting For A Sunny Day

(sung to the tune of "This Old Man")

Drip, drop, drop. Drip, drop, drop.
Will these raindrops ever stop?
I guess we'll wait for another sunny day.
Then we'll go outside to play!

Deborah Garmon, Groton, CT

I'm A Little Raindrop

Introduce youngsters to the water cycle with this simple song.

(sung to the tune of "I'm A Little Teapot")

I'm a little raindrop, wet and round,
Up in a cloud, far from the ground.

I'm a little raindrop, here I go,
Down to a puddle far below.

I'm a little raindrop, in the sun.
Changing to steam is so much fun!

I'm a little raindrop, rising in the heat.
Back to a cloud, isn't that neat?

I'm a little raindrop, wet and round,
Up in a cloud, far from the ground.

adapted from a song by Ronda Rasmussen—Preschool
Learning Ladder Preschool, La Mesa, CA

Out Pop The Raindrops!

(sung to the tune of "Pop! Goes The Weasel")

All around the sky today,
The clouds are full of raindrops.
They push and shove until they burst.
Out pop the raindrops!

Patricia Moeser—Toddlers
University of Wisconsin Preschool Laboratory
Madison, WI

49

Jelly-Bean Jamboree!
Sweet Ways To Learn Colors

Jumping jelly beans! Here's an assortment of ideas for teaching colors in a most delicious way—with jelly beans, the favorite candy of the season.

ideas contributed by dayle timmons

Bet You Can't Eat Just One!

Jelly beans might come in a variety of pretty colors, but they weren't made to admire. They were made for eating! Open a bag of jelly beans and invite each child in the group to take one. Ask each child to hold up his jelly bean when you name its color. Once each child is sure of his bean's color, have him eat it! Then sing this silly song. As each different color word is substituted, encourage the children who ate a bean of that color to stand up and rub their tummies. Ready for Round Two?

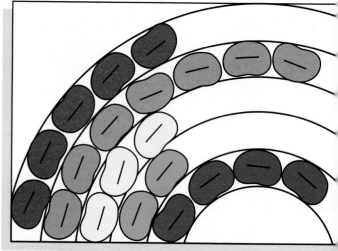

A Rainbow Of Colors

After several rounds of the previous song, your youngsters might have picked favorite flavors. Use this graphing idea to find out what they are. To prepare a graph on a length of white bulletin-board paper, draw a rainbow that has a segment for each different color of jelly bean in your package. Duplicate a supply of the jelly-bean patterns (page 55) onto construction paper that corresponds to each of the colors of your jelly beans. Cut out the jelly-bean shapes. Ask each child to pick a paper jelly-bean shape that represents his favorite flavor; then personalize the shape.

During a group time, return the shapes to the children. Sort the children by the colors of beans they selected; then help each child glue his shape to the rainbow to create a graph. Discuss the results. Celebrate your findings by eating—what else?—more jelly beans!

Jelly Beans In My Tummy!
(sung to the tune of "Skip To My Lou")

[Red] jelly beans—yum, yum.
[Red] jelly beans—yum, yum.
[Red] jelly beans—yum, yum.
Jelly beans in my tummy!

Colorful Stamping

Your little ones will be amazed—and you will be, too—over these stamps made from real jelly beans. To make two stamps, cut a large jelly bean in half lengthwise. Hot-glue each half to the bottom of a separate film canister so that its flat side can be used for printing. Make the desired number of stamps or make a pair of jelly-bean stamps for each different color of beans in your package. Provide shallow containers of paints that correspond to the colors of the beans. Cut out a large, white construction-paper jelly-bean shape for each child. Encourage each child to use the stamps to make prints on a cut-out shape.

As Colorful As Jelly Beans

Have interested children who are also fellow jelly-bean lovers help you make this book describing the variety of jelly-bean colors. In advance, cut out a supply of large jelly bean shapes. During a group time, ask your children to help you make lists of items that are the same colors as the colors of jelly beans in a package. When the lists have been made, give each child one of the bean-shaped pages. Ask him to choose a crayon that corresponds with one of the jelly-bean colors; then have him use the crayon to draw an item from the list or a different item of his choice. Write as he dictates his completion to the sentence shown. When each child has completed a page, sort the pages by color. Bind all the pages between similarly shaped tagboard covers. (If desired, use the printing method described in "Colorful Stamping" to decorate the covers of the book before assembling the pages.) Title the book. Soon your little ones will be hungry to read it all by themselves!

A __blue__ jelly bean is as __blue__ as __eyes__.

Jelly-Bean Countdown

Real jelly beans are so colorful, it doesn't take long for them to get eaten! Have your little ones help you count down the disappearing colors of jelly beans in this flannelboard rhyme. To prepare, use the patterns on page 55 to cut five different colors of felt jelly-bean shapes. Get ready! Count down!

Five little jelly beans;
I wish I had more!
I'll eat the [color word] one;
Now there are four.

Four little jelly beans;
Tasty as can be.
I'll eat the [color word] one;
Now there are three.

Three little jelly beans;
Only a few.
I'll eat the [color word] one;
Now there are two.

Two little jelly beans;
Eating them is fun.
I'll eat the [color word] one;
Now there is one.

One little jelly bean;
The last one for me.
I'll eat the [color word] one;
I'm as happy as can be!

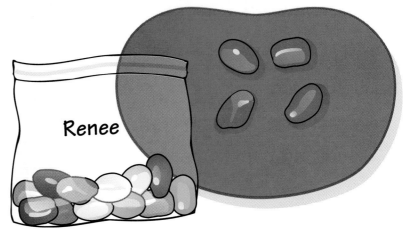

Assorted Colors

Tempt youngsters' taste buds with this colorful sorting activity. For each different color of jelly bean in a package, duplicate a jelly-bean pattern (page 55) onto a corresponding color of construction paper. Cut out the shapes; then place them in a center along with a class supply of personalized resealable plastic bags filled with jelly beans. To use the center, a child finds his bag of beans. He then places one of each different color of paper jelly-bean shape in front of him and sorts the matching real beans onto the shapes. No need to put *all* of those beans back in his bag when he's finished! Nibbling on the manipulatives is the treat for a sorting job well done.

Spilled Beans

A tisket, a tasket; fill a basket with colorful jelly beans! Here's a movement game that keeps youngsters actively identifying colors. To prepare, duplicate the jelly-bean patterns (page 55) onto various colors of construction paper so that the total number of beans is about three times the number of children in your class. Cut out the shapes; then laminate them for durability. To play, arrange the shapes on the floor in a circle. Put a basket in the middle of the circle. Invite your class to hop, tiptoe, or otherwise move beside the circular jelly-bean path as you sing the first verse of the following song. At the end of that verse, direct each child to place a foot on the nearest bean. Then sing the second verse to direct those children whose feet are on the named color of bean to drop those beans in the basket. Continue singing until all of the beans are in the basket.

Pick Up The Beans
(sung to the tune of "The Pawpaw Patch")

Moving around our jelly-bean circle.
Moving around our jelly-bean circle.
Moving around our jelly-bean circle.
What color jelly beans do you see?

Pick up the [color word] beans; put them in the basket.
Pick up the [color word] beans; put them in the basket.
Pick up the [color word] beans; put them in the basket.
Let's count the [color word] beans—you and me!

Soda Surprise

Plop, plop, fizz, fizz. What a thrill this soda is! Pour clear carbonated drink (such as Sprite® or 7-Up®) into as many ice-cube tray sections as you have children in your class. Ask each child to choose a color of jelly bean, name its color, and drop it into a section. Freeze the cubes. (The jelly beans' colors will tint the liquid to create colored cubes. Jelly Belly® jelly beans will not work for this activity.) During a snacktime, put a cube into a clear plastic cup for each child. Have each child find a cube that corresponds to the color of bean he selected; then assist him in filling his cup with the same type of clear soda used to make the cubes. As they watch the ice melt, youngsters will be surprised to see the clear soda blush with color. Using a spoon, remove the colorless bean from each child's drink. Wow! Drinks that taste like jelly beans!

Roly-Poly Beans

What happens when jelly-bean colors collide? Use jelly beans in this variation of marble painting to find out! To paint with jelly beans, select two different colors of jelly beans. Place a large, white construction-paper bean shape inside a tray. Carefully dip each jelly bean into a corresponding color of paint; then drop it onto the tray. Roll the jelly beans around the tray to create a design on the bean shape. Roly-poly jelly beans create cool art!

Jelly-Bean Stew For Me And You!

Colorful jelly beans are the main ingredient in this stew that reviews colors. Obtain several bags of jelly beans that include the colors listed in the following poem. Sort the beans by color; then divide them into sandwich bags so that each child has a bag of same-colored beans. Place a large pot in the center of your group. Introduce the poem to the children; then invite them to help you make jelly-bean stew. As you slowly repeat the poem, have each child pour his beans into the pot when his color of beans is named. Invite volunteers to stir the stew as you continue to repeat the poem. Using a soup ladle, fill a small cup with beans for each child. Let's all eat stew!

Jelly-Bean Stew

Jelly-bean stew,
Jelly-bean stew,
Red and yellow,
And purple, too!
Orange and pink,
And black and green,
It's the prettiest stew I've ever seen!

poem by Gloria Trabacca, Portland, OR

54

Jelly-Bean Patterns

Use with "A Rainbow Of Colors" on page 50, "Jelly-Bean Countdown" and "Assorted Colors" on page 52, and "Spilled Beans" on page 53.

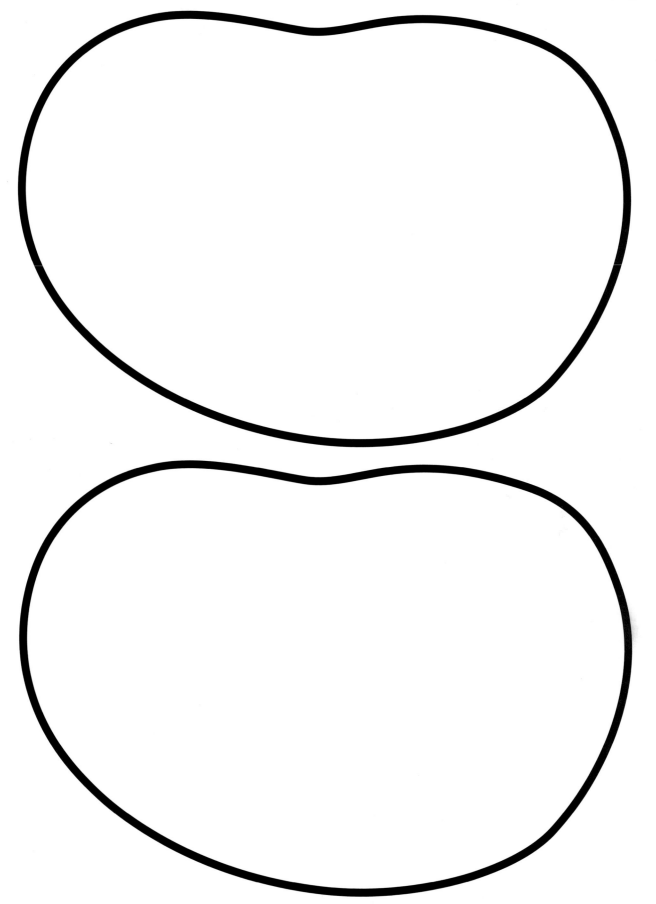

Wild About Watermelons!

Now that it's summer, you'll need juicy, mouthwatering, fresh-picked ideas to keep the learning growing. We think these ideas will be just "ripe"!

Pam Crane

Learning Your Way Around A Watermelon

It turns out that there's a lot of learning to be done with a watermelon. Watermelons aren't just for eating anymore—they're for learning about opposites, too. Take your children outside on a sunny day. Put a watermelon on newspaper on the ground. Begin your discussion about opposites by describing the *outside* of the watermelon. Ask volunteers what the *inside* will look like. Invite each child to thump the outside and try to pick up the watermelon. Next cut each child a slice. Compare the *soft* flesh of the inside to the *hard* rind of the outside. Discuss that while the whole watermelon was *heavy*, each slice is *light*. Best of all, eat your juicy slices. (Save those seeds and rinds! You'll need them for activities in this unit.) Mmmm, delicious and messy! Isn't *wet* better than *dry?*

LeeAnn Collins—Director, Sunshine House Preschool, Lansing, MI

Can A Watermelon Grow In My Tummy?

What's that? Someone swallowed a seed? Have no fear! The following song reminds little ones that a watermelon can't grow in there! Invite the children to echo you as you shout, "Oh, no!", then sing each verse.

Watermelon Echo Song
(sung to the tune of "Frère Jacques")

Oh, no! *(Oh, no!)*
I just swallowed *(I just swallowed)*
A watermelon seed. *(A watermelon seed.)*
Will I grow a watermelon *(Will I grow a watermelon)*
Deep in me? *(Deep in me?)*

Shout phrase, hands on face in alarm.
Begin singing slowly as with fear.

Oh, no! *(Oh, no!)*
That seed won't grow *(That seed won't grow)*
In my tummy. *(In my tummy.)*
There's no rain or sunshine *(There's no rain or sunshine)*
Deep in me! *(Deep in me!)*

Shout phrase.
Sing faster with joy.

LeeAnn Collins

A Tale Of Many Tendrils

Of course watermelon seeds can't sprout in tummies, but what *do* they need to grow vines and produce melons? Make this prop to describe the sequence of how a watermelon grows. Paint the bottoms of two paper plates green to resemble watermelons. Tape one end of a five-foot, green crepe-paper streamer to the inside rim of one plate. Starting near the opposite end of the streamer, glue a construction-paper yellow flower, then a green melon bud. Staple the rims of the plates together several times, leaving an opening opposite the end where the streamer is attached to the plate. Tuck the streamer into the watermelon pocket. As you share the following song or poem, gently pull the streamer vine out of the watermelon pocket, revealing the flower and then the melon bud.

Growing Melons

(sung to the tune of "The Farmer In The Dell")

Watermelon seeds, watermelon seeds,
On the ground and all around,
Watermelon seeds.

The vines begin to grow...

The yellow flowers bloom...

The melon buds appear...

Big and green and round, big and green and round,
The melons grow until they are all
Big and green and round.

Sharon Nichols, Madison Primary, Madison, FL

The Watermelon Story

A farmer plants a seed one day
And waits for it to grow.
Rain and sun and sandy soil
Are sure to help, you know.

A sprout pops up from underground,
Green as green can be.
It grows and grows so very long,
It's now a vine, you see.

A flower grows upon the vine,
Big and bright and new.
And right behind each lovely flower
Grows a watermelon, too!

The melons grow and grow and grow
Until they're big and grand.
They sit upon the farmer's field,
The best in all the land.

LeeAnn Collins—Director
Sunshine House Preschool
Lansing, MI

"Melondramatic" Play

Now that your little lip smackers have whet their appetites for watermelon and know what it takes to make one grow, prepare this patch for some dramatic play. Set the scene with props, such as a toy wheelbarrow, a watering can, three-foot lengths of hose, gardening gloves, garden tools, and straw hats. Label laundry baskets with pictures and signs labeled "small" and "large." Cover the patch with crepe-paper-streamer vines. What about the watermelons? Follow these instructions (right) for making papier-mâché melons. Be sure to invite each of your farmers to join you in the melon-making mania!

LeeAnn Collins—Director
Sunshine House Preschool, Lansing, MI

Mix warm water into an amount of flour until you have a thick, soupy paste.

Tearing along the grain, tear newspaper into one-inch-wide strips.

Blow up a balloon; then tie the end in a knot.

Repeatedly dip strips of newspaper into the paste; then press them onto the balloon.

Cover the balloon but not the knot.

When the paper is dry, cut off the knot; then remove the balloon.

Paint the shape to resemble a watermelon.

Surprise Me With Seeds

It's harvesttime at the play-dough center! Wash a number of the leftover seeds from your introductory eating experience. Use your favorite recipe to prepare a batch of bright-red play dough. (To add a watermelon scent to your dough, add a package of sugar-free, watermelon-flavored gelatin to the dry ingredients before cooking the dough.) Hide the seeds in a batch of the dough. Encourage youngsters to finger through the dough in search of the seeds. To encourage youngsters to sculpt their own watermelon slices, make a batch of green play dough to add to the center along with circular cookie cutters and plastic knives. This fine-motor melon center is sure to be picked over and over again.

LeeAnn Collins

A Slice Of Summer Art

That play-dough center sure did make good use of the leftover seeds. If you don't mind, we'll also use the rinds! To prepare a painting center, layer three plastic plates with moistened paper towels. Brush green, red, and black paint onto the towels to create three colors of paint pads. Provide small sponges and watermelon rinds. Encourage a child to dip a rind onto the green pad, then press it onto a large sheet of paper to create designs. If desired, a child may press a rind print, then use the sponges to add red and black paint until his prints resemble a watermelon.

LeeAnn Collins—Director, Sunshine House Preschool, Lansing, MI

Mighty "Vine" Visors

Keep slicing and dicing the fun with this fresh-off-the-vine visor idea. To make one, paint a paper-plate half to resemble a watermelon slice. Laminate a 1 1/2" x 16" paper strip. When the paint is dry, staple the ends of the strip to the plate to create a visor. If a child is feeling especially wacky in his watermelon hat, offer to use face paint to paint small black seeds on his cheeks. You're really wild over watermelons now!

Mary Ledyard—Preschool, Holy Rosary Central Steubenville, OH

Ornamental Melons

These melons are fun to make and can be used as necklaces, magnets, or ornaments. To make two melon slices, roll some Crayola® Model Magic® non-toxic, air-drying modeling compound into a ball. Press the ball flat. Use a knife to cut the pancake shape in half, creating two slices. Poke a hole in each slice that will be a necklace or an ornament. Allow the slices to dry overnight. Then color the slices with markers or paint them. If desired, glue real seeds to the slices. Thread appropriate ribbon lengths through the holes to make necklaces or ornaments. Or glue magnets on the backs of the slices.

Rae Warfel, Youngworld Children's Center, Wexford, PA

Watermelon Hopscotch

Use these ideas indoors or outdoors to inspire some melon movement and patterning practice. To prepare an outdoor hopscotch game, use chalk to draw a number of watermelon slices in a row on a sidewalk. Alternate drawing one, then two seeds in each slice. Encourage a child to hop along the slices as in hopscotch, landing on one foot where there is one seed in a slice, then on two feet where there are two seeds in a slice.

To prepare an indoor version, prepare a number of construction-paper watermelon slices with one or two seeds. Laminate the slices; then secure them to the floor in a row, alternating the one-seed slices with the two-seed slices. A child hops along the slices as described. One, two, one, two, one, two…

Amy Reynolds, Merry Moppet Preschool, Belmont, CA

What A Site!

Perhaps you'd like some tasty watermelon treats. Or maybe you've been pondering how to grow a patch of melons. Here's an Internet site we recommend: All About Watermelons (http://www.watermelon.org)—a watermelon Web site posted by the National Watermelon Promotion Board. When you visit this site, you'll find lots of tasty recipes for kids, a pattern for a watermelon puppet, information about how to grow watermelons, and even information about watermelon festivals that may be taking place in your state this summer. Check it out!

Refreshing Reading

"What-a-melon!" That's what folks will say when they see this interesting addition to your reading center. Fill a wading pool with pink or red shredded paper or tissue paper. Toss in a handful of black paper seed shapes; then wind crepe-paper-streamer vines around the pool. Invite youngsters to settle in for some seedy reading. See the book titles on page 61 for some refreshing reading ideas.

Beth Bonow, Hollywood, FL

Watermelon-Seed Maracas

Introduce some rhythm into your watermelon unit with these marvelous maracas. Collect a class supply of empty film containers. To make a maraca, use a black marker to draw seeds on a 1 7/8" x 4" piece of red paper. Tape the paper around a container. Put a number of watermelon seeds in the container; then secure the lid. Encourage each child to experiment with the sound of his maraca by adding or taking away seeds. Shake your maracas to the beat of your favorite summer songs. Or invite your little ones to shake their maracas to the beat as you sing Raffi's "Down By The Bay" (*Singable Songs For The Very Young*) or read the book (published by Crown Books For Young Readers).

LeeAnn Collins—Director, Sunshine House Preschool, Lansing, MI

Worth The Wait

Jesse waited and waited and waited for a watermelon day. At the end of the summer, the day arrived. *Then* she had to wait some more—a ripe watermelon has "a whole summer's worth of heat inside it" and takes a while to get good and cold. Read aloud *Watermelon Day* by Kathi Appelt (Henry Holt And Company, Inc.). Then have a taste-test to determine if your youngsters agree that cold watermelon is worth waiting for. In advance cut enough bite-sized watermelon pieces so that each child can have several. Put half of the pieces in the refrigerator and keep half at room temperature. When the pieces have chilled, have each child eat some cold and some warm watermelon; then take a vote to discover which youngsters prefer. Chances are, either way they'll prefer to keep eating watermelon!

LeeAnn Collins

You're Invited To
A Watermelon Day!
Join us after lunch on
Friday for a
slice of summer!

Everybody's Yellin' For Watermelon

Why wait all summer for a watermelon day? Begin planning a gathering today and invite youngsters' parents to join in the fun. Prepare a class supply of construction-paper invitations similar to the one shown; then send them home to parents.

On your day, simply gather together to enjoy a cool summer snack. Or encourage children to share with their parents those centers and activities they have enjoyed during your watermelon unit. To make a watermelon piñata for your festivities, follow the papier-mâché directions on page 58. Fill the papier-mâché watermelon with watermelon-flavored candies. Seal the hole with tape. Suspend the piñata for play. When the piñata is broken, distribute the candies among the group. Everybody's yellin', "We love watermelon!"

Nancy M. Lotzer, Farmers Branch, TX

Bubble Magic

Mix a little soap with water and what do you get? A magical solution for good, clean fun! So take a deep breath and blow into a unit that is positively bubbling over with art, science, language, and movement discoveries!

ideas by Lucia Kemp Henry

The Magic Potion

1/8 cup dishwashing liquid
1 cup water

This simple solution and the bubble-blowing tools suggested below are all you'll need to burst into bubble-blowing mania. Consider mixing a personalized plastic container full of the solution for each child. Or create a laboratory for the serious study of bubbles by multiplying the soap and water amounts as needed to fill a water table full of the solution. Place the water table outside along with these bubble-blowing tools made from inexpensive and easy-to-find household items. Students are sure to be delighted to discover that they can create billions and billions of bubbles!

What is a bubble?
A bubble is air trapped inside a ball of liquid.

Magic Wands And Bubble Blowers

Loop-And-Handle Wand
Twist a pipe cleaner as shown. Dip the loop into the bubble solution and blow through the opening or wave the wand in the air.

Fly Swatters
Dip a plastic fly swatter into the bubble solution; then wave it through the air.

Six-At-A-Time Bubble Wand
Tape a set of plastic, soda-can rings to one end of a dowel. Dip the rings in the bubble solution; then wave them through the air.

Bubble Straws
Cut a drinking straw in half; then cut the tip four times as shown. Dip the cut tip of the straw in the bubble solution. Gently blow through the clean end of the straw.

Spool Blowers
Soak an empty, plastic spool in warm water to remove the label. Dip one end of the spool in the bubble solution; then gently blow through the other end.

Bubble Tubes
Cut cardboard tubes into three-inch lengths. Dip one end of a tube in the bubble solution. Blow gently through the other end.

Catch Me, Catch Me, If You Can!

As students discover the magic of bubbles, ask them what they think bubbles are made of, how they float, and why they pop. Then suggest a simple experiment. Make sure that each child's hands are clean and dry. Ask the children to stand in front of you. Using a bubble-blowing tool that will create a bountiful supply of bubbles at one time, blow bubbles toward the children. Suggest that they attempt to catch the bubbles with their upturned hands. Then have them describe what happened when they attempted to catch the bubbles.

Next have youngsters wet their hands before standing in front of you. Once again, blow a supply of bubbles toward the children and encourage them to catch the bubbles. Was it easier to catch a bubble with wet hands?

Finally, moisten each child's palms with a small amount of bubble solution. Blow the bubbles toward the children, encouraging them to catch any bubbles that come their way. As the children discuss the results of this third round of bubble blowing and catching, help them contrast the results with the previous two attempts.

Why do bubbles stay on my soapy hands?
Soap makes the water's surface stretchy.

Why do bubbles pop?
The soapy solution dries, releasing the air inside the bubble.

Bubbles All Around

Fresh out of bubble solution? Don't fret! Singing this action song to the tune of "Twinkle, Twinkle, Little Star" is the next best thing to catching the real thing.

Bubbles floating all around.	*Pretend to catch bubbles.*
Bubbles fat and bubbles round.	*Make a big circle with arms.*
Bubbles on my toes and nose.	*Point to toes; then point to nose.*
Blow a bubble...up it goes!	*Pretend to blow a bubble; then point up.*
Bubbles floating all around.	*Pretend to catch bubbles.*
Bub...bles fall...ing to...the...ground.	*Sing slowly and sink to the ground.*

Big, Beautiful Bubbles

The bigger the bubble, the better! To make a wand guaranteed to create big, beautiful bubbles, tie both ends of an eight-inch length of soft string to a ten-inch, thin wooden dowel. Dip the wand into a pan of the bubble solution. Slowly lift the bubble wand; then gently wave it from side to side. To create even bigger bubbles, increase the length of the string. This bubble wand is sure to be "pop-ular"!

Big Bubble Big Book

Bet you can't say Big Bubble Big Book fast three times! Well, if you tried, it's a sure sign that this activity is for you! Once your students have had an opportunity to blow and catch bubbles, have them dictate their experiences, observations, and discoveries in a big bubble big book. Have each child use white finger paint to paint a big bubble shape on a sheet of finger-paint paper. While the paint is wet, have her sprinkle ultrafine, multicolored glitter on the bubble. When the paint is dry, shake off the excess glitter. Cut around the circumference of the shimmering bubble; then glue the painted bubble on a large sheet of construction paper. Write on the paper as she dictates a sentence about bubbles. Bind the pages between covers to create a book. Then read the book aloud during a group time.

My bubbles floated all the way to the sky!
Sarah

The Shape Of Bubbles To Come

Yet another bubble discovery awaits your little ones with this simple experiment. Blow some bubbles using a standard bubble-blowing wand with a round opening. Ask your little ones to observe the shape of the bubbles as well as the shape of the wand. Then bend several plastic-coated hangers into different shapes. Ask youngsters to predict how the bubbles blown from these wands will be shaped. Blow the bubbles and discuss the results.

Why are bubbles rounded in shape?

The surface tension of the bubble solution pulls it inward. At the same time, the air inside the bubble is pushing out in all directions.

Bubble-Shaped Prints

With this group art activity, it really is circle time! Have your little ones gather around a large, bulletin-board-paper circle. Fill several meat trays with the same color of tempera paint; then set the trays on sheets of newspaper arranged outside the circle. Encourage youngsters to dip circular-shaped sponges and cardboard tubes into the paint, then press them onto the large circle. When the bubble-shaped prints are dry, replace the paint with a different color. Then invite students to gather around again for a second round of printing. Round and round and round we go!

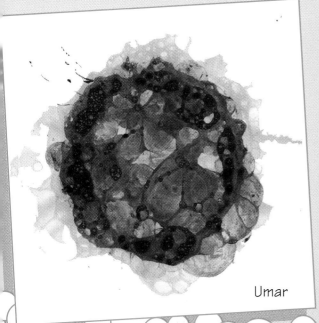

Umar

Pop Art

Capture the beauty of bubbles with this entertaining art project. Fill several plastic cups with water. Add several drops of dishwashing liquid and a spoonful of a different color of dry tempera paint to each cup of water. Stir the mixtures; then place the cups on a tray or towel. Provide each child with a straw and a personalized piece of white construction paper. To make pop art, a child uses his straw to blow air into a cup. When he has blown a fountain of bubbles, have him gently place his paper atop the bubbles. Repeat as desired to capture different colors of bubbles. Your little ones are sure to be blown away by the results!

Bubble Colors

The sky isn't the only place to spy a rainbow! There's a whole spectrum of colors on every bubble your little ones blow. To help children discover the colors on bubbles, invite them to join you in this activity. After seating the children on the floor, turn the lights off so that the lighting in your classroom is dim but not completely dark. Blow bubbles into the room; then ask the children to describe any colors they could see on the bubbles. Then take the class to a sunny area outside. Again blow bubbles and ask the children to describe the colors they could see. Have youngsters discuss the differences in the two rounds of bubble-blowing and give reasons for the appearance of colors on the bubbles when they were blown outside.

Why are there colors on a bubble?

When light shines through a bubble, the water bends the light and splits it into the colors of the rainbow.

A Rainbow In A Bubble

Let's look inside a bubble
To see if there might be
A few bright rainbow colors
For all of us to see.

Can you see red?
Can you see blue?
So many, many colors—
How do they look to you?

Can you see yellow?
Can you see green?
Aren't these pretty colors
The best you've ever seen?

Can you see purple?
Can you see rose?
How did such pretty colors
Get inside one of those?

How do bubbles get their colors?
Do you think you know?
Perhaps a rainbow lives inside
Each bubble that we blow!

—Lucia Kemp Henry

Watercolor Bubbles

After completing the activity described in "Bubble Colors," read the poem "A Rainbow In A Bubble" to your children. Ask volunteers to answer the questions posed in the poem. Then give each child an opportunity to record his discovery by painting watercolor bubbles. Provide each child with a sheet of painting paper on which a large circle has been traced. Have each child paint the circle with watercolor paints. When the paint is dry, cut out each child's circle. Mount all of the watercolor bubbles on a bulletin board along with a copy of the poem "A Rainbow In A Bubble."

Bubbles, Bubbles Everywhere!

Little ones are fascinated by the magic of bubbles floating through the air. Make these simple bubble projects to suspend from your ceiling and you'll add a bubbly touch to your classroom that will never pop or float away! To make a floating bubble, cut a circle from tagboard; then cut out a circle from the center. Squeeze glue along the edge of one side of the circle. Press a sheet of white tissue paper that is slightly larger than the circle onto the glue. Allow the glue to dry, then repeat the process on the other side of the circle. Trim the excess tissue paper from around the circle. Then splatter-paint both sides of the circle with light blue tempera paint. Punch a hole near the edge of the circle; then thread with clear fishing line. Tie a knot in the fishing line and suspend the circle from the ceiling. Bubbles, bubbles everywhere. Floating, floating in the air!

Why do bubbles float up?

Warm air is lighter than cold air. If the air you blow into a bubble is warmer than the air around you, the bubble will float up.

Double The Bubble Fun

The most magical thing about bubbles is that no matter how you blow them, you always end up with lots of fun! As a culminating activity, videotape your youngsters blowing bubbles. Take the class outside on a sunny day and provide them with plenty of the magic potion and the magic wands or bubble blowers described on page 62. Using a portable tape player, play the instrumental music of your choice. Film the class in action, being sure to get a close-up of each child. If desired, interview each child as he blows bubbles.

After watching the video as a class, prepare to send the video home by wrapping it in plastic bubble wrap. Place the wrapped video in a bag along with a loop-and-handle bubble-blowing wand and a copy of the bubble-solution recipe (see page 62). Also include a note encouraging parents to enjoy the video for several days and to keep the recipe and wand when returning the video, book, and bag to school. Replace the recipe and wand before sending the bag home with another child. Bubbles away!

We captured our bubble magic on video! When you have enjoyed the video and the book, please return them. Keep the recipe and wand for your own bubble fun!

"Bee" Polite!

Please allow me to introduce myself. I'm Miss Bea Polite, a queen bee of impeccable manners. May I help you keep your hive buzzing with good manners? Very well! Let's get started, shall we?

ideas contributed by Miss Bea Polite and Lisa D. Cowman

It's Nice To Meet You!

Get "buzzy" teaching your little ones about manners by making a Miss Bea look-alike. To make one, gather a nine-inch, orange foam ball; a straw hat; two black pipe cleaners; two practice golf balls; and black and pink Slick® fabric paints. To make Miss Bea's antennae, paint the plastic golf balls black. Fold each pipe cleaner in half and twist it. Insert one end of each pipe cleaner into a golf ball, and the other end into the top of the straw hat. Paint facial features on the foam ball. When the paint is dry, gently press the ball into the hat.

During a group time, bring Miss Bea out for a flyby. Modeling your most appropriate manners, introduce Miss Bea to each child by saying, "Miss Bea, this is [Child's name]. [Child's name], this is Miss Bea Polite." Encourage each child to respond by saying, "It's nice to meet you!" When all formal introductions have been made, explain to your group that your honored guest has arrived so that your class can learn about manners. Ask volunteers to explain what they think it means to be polite and have them give examples of good manners. If desired, record their examples. Then conclude by reminding your children that Miss Bea will be using her eyes and antennae to watch and listen for good manners in your classroom. When she does indeed observe politeness, allow her to buzz a word of praise in that child's ear.

Miss Bea's Recommended Reading

To help your little ones better understand mannerly behavior, Miss Bea Polite recommends reading aloud and discussing the following books:

Say Please
Written & Illustrated by Virginia Austin
Published by Candlewick Press

Perfect Pigs: An Introduction To Manners
Written & Illustrated by Marc Brown
and Stephen Krensky
Published by Little, Brown and Company

What Do You Say, Dear? and *What Do You Do, Dear?*
Written by Sesyle Joslin
Illustrated by Maurice Sendak
Published by HarperCollins Children's Books

Monster Manners
Written by Bethany Roberts
Illustrated by Andrew Glass
Published by Clarion Books

Mind Your Manners

If you'd like your little ones to begin making choices about mannerly behavior, keep this activity in mind. First have each child make a Miss Bea bee puppet. To make one, draw a smiling face on one yellow paper plate and a frowning face on a second plate. Color two craft sticks black. Cut two small circles from black construction paper; then glue a circle to one end of each craft stick to represent antennae. To the back of one plate, tape the craft-stick antennae at the top of the plate. Tape another craft stick to the bottom of the plate for a handle. Glue the backs of both plates together.

When each child has made a puppet, have him use his puppet during this group-time activity. Using each of the following suggestions, describe a situation in which proper or improper manners were used. Direct each child to display either the happy or sad expression on his puppet to indicate if Miss Bea Polite would approve or disapprove of the behavior. After using the following suggestions, encourage volunteers to contribute scenarios of their own.

Beatrice Butterfly said, "Pass the flowers, *please.*"
Gracie Grasshopper said, *"Thank you,"* when she was given a treat.
Bobby Bumblebee bumped his brother off the beehive.
Arnie Ant waited his turn in line.
Carl Caterpillar crunched quietly.
Chrysy Caterpillar chatted with her mouth full.
Sammy Spider played with his food.
Christopher Cricket chirped while another cricket was chirping.
Casey Cricket chirped, *"Excuse me,"* before interrupting.
Lucy Ladybug borrowed a leaf without asking.

A Honey Of A Game!

This honey of a game will give your little ones practice using the magic words "please" and "thank you." In advance, cut a honeycomb shape from yellow construction paper; then add details with a marker. Remove Miss Bea Polite's straw hat and place it in a chair that is near, but facing away from your group area. To play, seat the class on the floor. Ask a volunteer to sit in the chair, wear the hat, and pretend to be Miss Bea. Place the honeycomb under the chair. Ask Miss Bea to close her eyes; then quietly choose another child to tiptoe to the chair and take the honeycomb. The child then returns to the group and sits on the honeycomb. Ask Miss Bea to open her eyes and face the group. Recite this chant:

(Class)	Miss Bea Polite, you're very sweet.
	May we *please* have a honey treat?
(Miss Bea)	Miss Bea Polite says, "Yes, you may."
(Class)	*"Thank you, thank you,"* we all say.

Give Miss Bea several chances to guess who took the honeycomb before revealing the child, if necessary. The child who took the honeycomb then becomes the new Miss Bea. Continue play until each child has been the queen bee.

"Bee-utiful" Behavior

Miss Bea Polite recommends making a batch of these bee stickers to remind youngsters to use good manners. Or use the stickers as rewards for children who make an effort to show exceptional etiquette. Simply use a black marker to draw stripes on a set of yellow dot stickers. Encourage a child to press a sticker on his hand or clothing. Your room is sure to be buzzin' with "bee-utiful" behavior!

Sweet Table Manners

Place a container of Honeycomb® cereal in your housekeeping area along with napkins, small paper plates, and a spoon. Set Miss Bea on the center of your housekeeping table. Encourage each child at the center to have a seat at the table, obtain a napkin and a plate, and serve himself a spoonful of cereal. Remind youngsters that Miss Bea will be watching for polite table manners such as keeping mouths closed while chewing, using napkins to wipe mouths and hands, taking turns, saying "Please" and "Thank you," saying "Excuse me" before leaving the table, and cleaning up properly.

Tea-Party Time

Celebrate good manners with a tea party! To prepare for your party, collect dress-up items such as scarves, hats, and ties. Also purchase the ingredients, utensils, and paper supplies needed to make and enjoy honey buns and tea (directions below). Prepare a giant invitation from Miss Bea Polite; then ask an adult volunteer to deliver it to your class on the morning of the day you've planned for your party. Read the invitation aloud. Discuss the manners that will be necessary at the party, relating them to these opposites: clean/dirty, neat/messy, polite/rude, smile/frown, quiet/loud. Invite each child to dress up using the gathered items of clothing. Then let the celebration begin!

It's Tea Party Time! Come celebrate good manners with Miss Bea!

Honey Buns And Tea

Miss Bea suggests serving these treats at your tea party. Use any biscuit dough (including canned) and a small, round canapé cutter to make miniature biscuits. Bake the biscuits; then slice and top them with different kinds of honey (clover, sage, orange blossom, etc.). Accompany the biscuits with decaffeinated mint tea.

70

COLOR
and
SHAPE
Units

Splashes Of Red!

Colorful ideas to help your little ones experience the color red!

Colorful Literature

Introduce your youngsters to the color red by reading red-related literature and dressing for the occasion! Wear articles of red clothing while reading aloud the book *Red Is Best* by Kathy Stinson (Firefly Books, Ltd.). After reading, ask each youngster to look around the classroom for items that are red. Then have your children sit in a circle to play a game similar to Hot Potato. Show them a red apple. As you play a musical recording, have each student in turn pass the apple to the child sitting next to him. Stop the music periodically, and have the child holding the apple stand up and point out an item that is red.

Need some other splashes of red? Try these colorful, red-related books:

Mary Wore Her Red Dress & Henry Wore His Green Sneakers adapted and illustrated by Merle Peek (Clarion Books)

Is It Red? Is It Yellow? Is It Blue? by Tana Hoban (Greenwillow Books)

Who Said Red? written by Mary Serfozo and illustrated by Keiko Narahashi (Macmillan Children's Book Group)

Circle Time

Little ones will love this "color-rific" circle-time idea. While learning about the color red, ask each youngster to bring a small, red item from home in a paper bag. During circle time, have each youngster bring his paper bag to the circle. Ask a student to volunteer to give the rest of the class clues about the object in his bag. Encourage the rest of the students to ask questions about the object; then have them try to guess what it is. Have the student volunteer reveal what's in his bag. Continue in this manner until each child has had a turn.

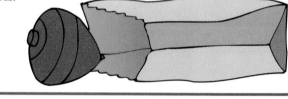

Really Red Fruit Salad

Stir up some colorful enthusiasm in your room by having youngsters create really red fruit salads. In advance, cut up pieces of red apples, cherries, watermelon, strawberries, and red grapes; then place each of the fruits in a different bowl. Place the bowls on a table. Provide each child with a red plastic spoon and a red cup. Encourage him to spoon the fruits of his choice from the bowls into his cup. Yum!

Red Day

Designate one day of the week to be Red Day. The day before, instruct youngsters to wear as many red articles of clothing as possible on Red Day. Then place a red stick-on dot on the back of each child's hand as a special reminder before he goes home. When this special day arrives, have your little ones discuss their red clothing with the rest of the class.

Centers With A Colorful Flair

- Try these quick-and-easy suggestions to help youngsters recognize the color red. Supply your math center with red poker chips, buttons, blocks, and other manipulatives. Have your little ones sort and classify the items by shape, size, and texture.

- Put a variety of red clothing in the dramatic play area, along with pictures or actual samples of red food items.

- Stock your art center with old magazines, scissors, red crayons, glue, and white construction paper. To use this center, have your students look through the magazines and cut out pictures of things that are red; then have them glue the pictures to the construction paper. A child may also choose to draw objects that are red. Now that's a red picture!

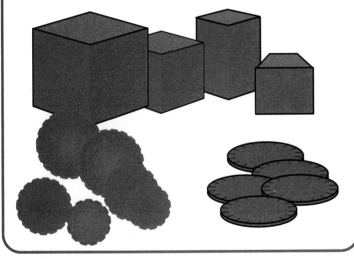

Moving Right Along

Select musical recordings carefully for this activity, and your youngsters will be color dancing in no time. Before starting the music, tape red crepe-paper streamers around each child's wrists. As you start the music, encourage your children to dance and move freely to the rhythm so that their streamers move expressively.

This looks like a flower. Katie

"Red-y" For Art?

- Your students will be caught red-handed with smiles of delight when making these creative collages. Supply each child with red craft items such as glitter, markers, glitter glue, sequins, ribbon, feathers, crayons, yarn, pom-poms, and tissue paper. Have each child glue the craft items of his choice onto a large sheet of white construction paper. After the glue dries, allow time for each child to talk about his special collage.

- On another day, have each child place a dab of red paint inside a folded sheet of white construction paper. Refold the paper. Starting at the fold, have each child push the paint out toward the edges of his paper. Then have him open the folded paper to see his design. Have each child dictate a sentence about his design, as you write the sentence at the bottom of his paper.

- When your little ones do this red art activity, it will not only prove to be lots of fun, but your room will smell fresh and clean too. In advance, cover your tabletops with white bulletin-board paper. Squeeze a dab of shaving cream in front of each child; then add 1/4 teaspoon of red water-based paint or red powdered tempera paint to the shaving cream. Using his fingers, have each child mix the shaving cream and paint. Encourage each child to finger-paint with the red shaving cream, making the designs of his choice.

Judy Jones—Preschool; Get Ready, Set, Grow; Boca Raton, FL

73

Splashes Of Orange

Colorful ideas to help your little ones experience the color orange!

Color Of Autumn

Roll up your sleeves. Pass out the art smocks. It's time to be up to your elbows in orange paint! To introduce the color orange, scoop large dollops of red and yellow finger paint onto a clean tabletop. Mist the tabletop with water. Encourage several students at a time to take turns smearing the two colors of paint to blend them. Monitor this process to stimulate discussions about what is happening to the paint and to mist the table whenever it becomes too dry. When youngsters have tired of finger-painting, press a giant, white, bulletin-board paper leaf cutout onto the table. Smooth it down; then carefully lift it up and place it where it can dry. Repeat this process several times, if desired, to "colorize" several giant leaf cutouts and to give each youngster an opportunity to mix red and yellow to get orange. Later post the leaves with student-dictated thoughts about things that become orange in autumn.

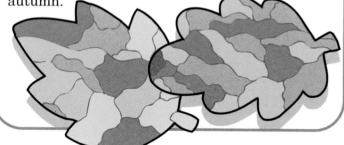

Orange Floats

A scoop of orange sherbet is the main ingredient in this irresistible drink. Lead into this activity by having students brainstorm foods and beverages that are orange. Ask students to tell what their favorite orange foods are. Slice or peel three or four oranges while the youngsters watch. As you discuss the color, smell, and taste of the fruit, have your preschoolers help you separate the oranges into sections. Put a scoop of orange sherbet in a small cup for each youngster. Then assist as each child pours some orange soda into the cup, garnishes the drink with a section of orange, and inserts a straw. While students are sipping their orange drinks, make it more of a festive occasion by singing the song in "Orange Sillies."

Orange Sillies

While students are sipping their orange floats (described above), lead them in singing a silly orange song. In the first four lines of the song, sing one phrase at a time, pausing for students to echo or repeat the phrase (indicated by italics), before singing the phrase on the next line.

Sippin'
(sung to the tune of "The Silliest Goat I Ever Saw")

The silliest girl (boy); *The silliest girl (boy)*
I ev-er saw; *I ev-er saw*
Was sip-pin' or-; *Was sip-pin' or-*
'Ange through a straw; *'Ange through a straw.*
The silliest girl (boy) I ev-er saw
Was sip-pin' o-range through a straw!

Outside Art

If your playground has a chain-link fence, you've got a great canvas for an orange weaving. To prepare for this activity, cut an orange fabric remnant (or an old sheet that has been dyed orange) into long, three-inch-wide strips. Also provide several similar strips of fabrics of different colors. In your collection, include assorted items that are orange. For example, you may include orange feathers, a string of plastic orange beads, some orange rickrack, or orange clothespins. Store the strips and other orange items in a laundry basket. Take your little ones outside and show them how to weave the strips in and out through the sections of the chain-link fence. Then let the creativity begin! Encourage students' participation in the weaving, but otherwise let the artwork evolve according to the preferences of the children. It's not necessary that the weaving resemble anything in particular. But when it's finally finished, you can step back and admire one thing for sure. That is really orange art!

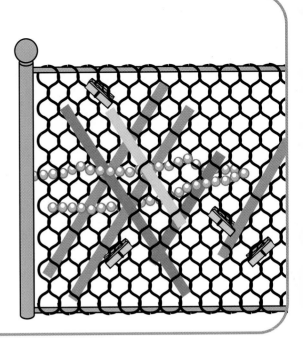

Orange Blossoms

Put out the word. Your class is on the lookout for orange papers and fabrics of all kinds. To get started, show students a few orange things that you have gathered. For example, you might have a remnant of orange cloth, sheets of several orange papers, and a woven orange produce bag. Explain that you are donating these things for a class project; then drop them into a collection bin labeled "orange." Encourage students to contribute to the orange box during the next few days.

When you have an adequate collection, cut the fabrics and papers into one-inch-wide strips. Provide each student with scissors, craft glue, and an 18-inch circle of white poster board. Have the youngster cut and glue strips of her choice to the circle to make a bright orange flower. Display each of the flowers along a classroom wall with paper leaves and stems of varying heights. What an amazing fall flower bed!

Orange Memories

Culminate your celebration of the color orange by setting aside a day to be Orange Day. Ask that on this day, each of the children wears something that is orange. (Have on hand a box of orange accessories—such as badges, hats, and shoestrings—for youngsters who forget about Orange Day.) Once everyone is all decked out in orange, invite them to look in a full-length mirror, then draw their likenesses on art paper. Help each student complete a fill-in-the-blank sentence about the orange clothing he is wearing. Then use masking tape to bind the artwork into a booklet with an orange-embellished cover.

M. Lynne Sypher, Brook Avenue School, Bay Shore, NY

Splashes Of Green

Colorful ideas to help your little ones experience the color green!

Green From Tip To Tail

Watch out! With this art project, you'll have a slithery, sneaky snake that changes colors. To make a giant snake, you'll need a large piece of finger-painting paper for each child. Tape the papers together, end to end, to create one long strip. Trim along the top and bottom of the strip in a wavy manner, so that it resembles a snake. Using permanent markers, create features and attach a red construction-paper tongue. Spread the snake shape out in a long, uncarpeted hallway or on a long strip of plastic. On each child's section of paper, drop a dollop of blue and yellow finger paint. Then invite several children at a time to put on art smocks and finger-paint their sections of the paper snake. When all sections have been painted and have dried, mount the snake on the wall.

It's A Jungle In There!

Surround your youngsters with the color green by transforming your classroom into a growing green room. Set the mood by draping your cabinets, shelves, and windows with artificial greenery. During a group time, ask your little ones to brainstorm a list of things that can be green. Write each child's suggestion on a large, light green paper leaf shape. Then ask each child to illustrate his suggestion on his leaf with crayons or paints. Mount the illustrated leaf shapes onto slightly larger, dark green paper leaf shapes. Attach each leaf to a green, crepe-paper streamer and suspend it from the ceiling. Now you're growing wild with green!

Grapes are green. Samuel

Dip And Nibble

By now your youngsters have been surrounded with green for viewing and have been up to their elbows in green for touching. What's next in experiencing the color green? Tasting, of course! On your next trip to the grocery store, shop for an assortment of green vegetables such as broccoli, celery, green peppers, zucchini, and cucumbers. (Or ask parents to contribute these vegetables.) Cut the green veggies into portions just right for preschoolers to dip and nibble on. (Save some of the vegetables for "Tossed-Salad Art.") Add green food coloring to ranch dressing; then pour the dressing into small cups or bowls. Provide each child with a cup of the dressing for dipping the vegetables of his choice.

Tossed-Salad Art

Using the green vegetables suggested in "Dip And Nibble," have students make vegetable prints. In an art center, place the cut vegetables and a pie tin of green paint. Provide each child in the center with a white paper plate. Encourage her to dip one of the vegetables in the paint and press it onto the plate. Have her repeat this process using the various vegetables. To create a display, cover a table with a green paper tablecloth. Tape the dry vegetable prints to the tablecloth along with a sign titled "Tossed-Salad Art."

Adapted from an idea by
  Suzanne Costner
  Maryville, TN

Green Giggles And Jiggles

Make a batch of lime-flavored Jell-O® Jigglers® gelatin snacks, and you are sure to hear lots of giggles from your little ones. To make the gelatin snacks, follow the directions on a package of lime-flavored Jell-O® brand gelatin. Then provide youngsters with cookie cutters in the shapes of Christmas trees, dinosaurs, and other things that can be green. Assist each child in using the cutter of his choice to cut out a gelatin snack. If desired, provide whipped topping that has been tinted green and green sprinkles for topping the treats. Watch them wiggle! See them jiggle!

The Grass Is Greener

The ground might be covered with snow outside, but in your class the grass is green and growing. Collect a class supply of half-pint milk cartons. Clean the cartons and cut off their tops. Provide each child with a strip of paper cut to match the height of the carton and long enough to wrap around it. Have each child paint his strip green. While the paint is wet, have him sprinkle the strip with green glitter. When it's dry, tape or glue the strip around a carton. Assist each child in filling his carton with soil. Have him gently press a spoonful of birdseed into the dirt. Place the cartons by a window and watch the green grass grow.

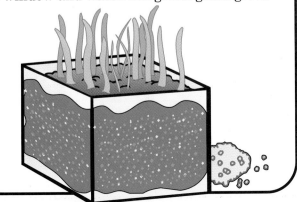

"It's Not Easy Being Green"

Bring your celebration of the color green to a close by listening to everyone's favorite frog sing "Bein' Green." A recording of the song can be found on *Sesame Street Platinum: All Time Favorites* (Sony/Wonder). If possible, manipulate a frog puppet while playing the song.

Splashes Of Purple

Colorful ideas to help your little ones experience the color purple!

Welcome To Purpleville

Introduce your youngsters to the color purple by transforming your classroom into Purpleville. Before students arrive, embellish your classroom cabinets, windows, and shelves with purple streamers, curling ribbon, and inflated balloons. Cover each table or desk with purple bulletin-board paper. Place a vase filled with artificial purple flowers and a purple paper plate with purple grapes on each desk or table. On the front of your classroom door, tape a sign that reads "Welcome To Purpleville." As your little ones enter, lead them in singing the following song. Have youngsters substitute a different action each time the verse is sung.

WELCOME TO PURPLEVILLE

The Land Of Purpleville
(sung to the tune of "Here We Go Round The Mulberry Bush")

In the land of Purpleville,
The children there wear purple still.
They love to dance and they love to sing,
And they love to [clap their hands].

Jean Harrison
Palm Bay, FL

78

Purple Pizzazz

These purple foods have lots of pizzazz. Begin by having your youngsters brainstorm purple foods. Have a few food items such as an eggplant, purple grapes, beets, and red cabbage on hand to display and discuss. After the discussion, ask youngsters to name beverages that are purple. Then show them a bottle of grape soda. For each child, put a scoop of vanilla ice cream in a purple cup. Then assist as each child pours some grape soda into the cup and garnishes the ice cream with purple cake sprinkles. "Purple-licious!"

Color Me A Cookie

Try this sweet idea for some colorful fun. Bake sugar cookies from refrigerated dough according to the package directions. When the cookies have cooled, provide each group of children with cookies, plastic knives, and a small bowl of purple icing (use icing in a tube or add purple concentrated paste to vanilla icing). Encourage each child to cover his cookie with the purple icing. Then have each child top off his cookie with a dab of grape jelly, if desired, and enjoy it!

A Royal Show-And-Tell

Your students will feel like kings and queens with this royal idea. In advance paint a medium-size box and its lid purple. When the paint is dry, stock a center with the box, scissors, glue, and purple craft items such as yarn, ribbon, pom-poms, fake jewels, sequins, lace, feathers, felt pieces, and tissue-paper pieces. Then let the decorating begin! Encourage youngsters to embellish the box with the provided items so that it resembles a royal treasure chest.

Later designate one day to be Royal Show-And-Tell Day. On the day before, encourage each child to wear something that is purple and to bring in a purple object from home. As each child enters the classroom on this special day, have him place his purple object in the decorated treasure chest. During show-and-tell, seat your youngsters in a circle on the floor and place the chest in the middle of the circle. In turn, crown each child with a purple construction-paper crown and place a piece of purple cloth around his shoulders to represent a royal cloak. Then have each child describe his purple object without naming it. Have the rest of the class try to guess what the object is before it is revealed.

Jean Harrison
Palm Bay, FL

Ready To Make Purple?

Your little artists will love letting their creative juices flow with this fun idea. On a clean table in front of each child, place dabs of red and blue washable paint. Ask him what he thinks will happen when the two colors are mixed. Using his hands, have each student mix the two colors together. Encourage each child to use his fingers to make the design of his choice in the paint. When each child is satisfied with his creation, gently place a sheet of white construction paper atop his design. Rub your hand lightly over the entire paper. Lift the paper and let the paint dry.

After having each of your youngsters share their prints, have them sing the following song, substituting a different action each time the verse is sung:

If You Like The Color Purple

(sung to the tune of "If You're Happy And You Know It")

If you like the color purple, [clap your hands].
  Clap twice.
If you like the color purple, [clap your hands].
  Clap twice.
You can make the color true,
By mixing red and blue;
If you like the color purple, [clap your hands].
  Clap twice.

Jean Harrison

How Now, Purple Cow?

Here's a "moo-velous" idea for reviewing the color purple. In advance, use a purple marker or chalk to copy Gelette Burgess's "The Purple Cow" (from memory or a poetry book such as *Favorite Poems Old And New* edited by Helen Ferris) on a chalkboard or piece of chart paper. Ask your students if they have ever seen a purple cow. Graph the results and discuss what the graph reveals. Read the poem aloud; then let students volunteer to share their reactions to the poem. Read the poem several more times, having youngsters join in as they are able. Then give each child a cow-shaped cutout (pattern on page 96) and have him decorate it using art supplies such as purple construction-paper scraps, crayons, glitter, tissue-paper pieces, and buttons.

Splashes Of Yellow

Colorful ideas to help your little ones experience the color yellow!

Yellow, Yellow, Everywhere!

Brainstorm a list of yellow things with your youngsters. Then sing this bright and cheery song to the tune of "Twinkle, Twinkle, Little Star."

Yellow, yellow, bright and fair;
Yellow, yellow, everywhere.
Lemonade and apples, too;
Golden yellow hair on you.
Yellow, yellow, bright and fair;
Yellow, yellow, everywhere.

Tracy Lynn Troup—Pre-K

When Life Gives You Lemons

Make lemon prints and lemonade! In advance cut a quantity of lemons in half lengthwise. Set several of the lemon halves aside to dry slightly. Store the remaining halves in a refrigerator. Then, in an art center, place the lemon halves, white construction paper, newspaper, and a pan of yellow tempera paint. Encourage each child to dip a lemon half in the paint, press it onto the newspaper, and then press it onto a sheet of construction paper. Have him continue in this manner until he has several prints on his paper. As a nifty follow-up activity, make lemonade with the leftover lemons!

Tracy Lynn Troup—Pre-K

Tasty Graphing

Stir up some excitement in your room when graphing youngsters' favorite yellow foods. Using yellow paper, create a graph with the name and picture of each yellow food that will be tasted. Place a variety of yellow foods—such as bananas, cheese, corn, scrambled eggs, macaroni and cheese, and corn bread—on a table. Provide each child with a yellow plate and a plastic spoon. Have each child place a portion of each food on his plate, and encourage him to taste each food. Supply each child with a personalized, yellow happy-face cutout. Have each student indicate his favorite yellow food by placing his happy face in the appropriate place on the graph. Ask questions such as "How many children like cheese the best?" and "Do more people like bananas or cheese?"

Tracy Lynn Troup—Pre-K
Family Day Care/Preschool
Lebanon, PA

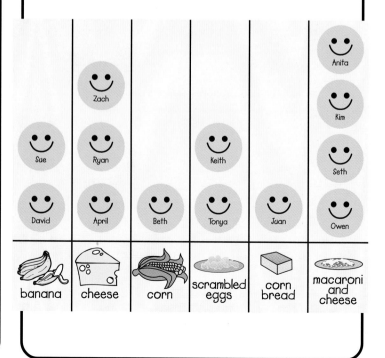

Yellow Mellow Butter

Read aloud *Brown Cow, Green Grass, Yellow Mellow Sun* by Ellen Jackson (Hyperion Books for Children). Spread out the fun of the story by having your youngsters make yellow mellow butter. To make butter, provide each child with a small, plastic jar half filled with room-temperature whipping cream. Secure the lid on each jar. Have each child shake, shake, shake, until the cream is yellow mellow butter. Provide each child with a plastic knife and a slice of bread, and have him spread some of his homemade butter atop the bread. Yum!

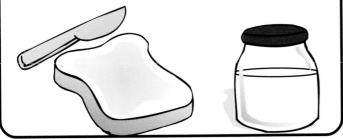

Yellow, Yellow, Friendly Fellow

Keep a small, round, yellow pillow in a prominent place for your students to hold when they are feeling gloomy. When a child needs a little extra attention, encourage him to hold the yellow, yellow, friendly fellow pillow. Remind the class to give that student some tender loving care for the day.

Kathy Mulvihill—Four-Year-Olds
Wee Care Preschool
Allendale, MI

You Are My Sunshine

These suns will make you happy when skies are gray. Provide each child with a tagboard circle cutout and yellow tissue-paper pieces. Have each student glue the tissue paper onto the tagboard so that the pieces overlap to cover the circle. Then have each youngster drizzle yellow or gold glitter glue atop the tissue paper. When the glue is dry, glue several yellow streamers to the edge of the circle to resemble a sun. Encourage each of your little ones to hold his sun cutout above his head while singing "You Are My Sunshine" or while listening to Raffi's "One Light, One Sun."

The Yellow Pages

Need a unique art technique? Look in the yellow pages! Reuse old telephone books by removing the yellow pages. Encourage youngsters to tear or cut the pages, then glue them to black construction paper. You'll be able to call these collages one-of-a-kind!

Literature Links

Yellow Ball
Written & Illustrated by Molly Bang
(Out of print. Check your library.)

Little Blue And Little Yellow
Written & Illustrated by Leo Lionni
Published by Mulberry Books

Splashes Of Blue

Fun and colorful ideas to help your little ones experience the color blue!

Blueberries For You

Introduce the color blue with this "berry" nice idea. On a designated day, ask youngsters to wear as many articles of blue clothing as possible. Ask them to bring a toy bear to school on the same day. Upon students' arrival, seat them in a group and read aloud *Blueberries For Sal* by Robert McCloskey (Puffin Books). Explain that since everyone has a bear, it must be time for berry picking. All you need are berry buckets.

To make a bucket for each child, fold down several inches of a closed, white paper bag. Cut a half-circle shape through all thicknesses; then unfold and open the bag. Program each bag with the phrase "Blueberry Bucket." Have each child paint a green bush on his bag. Next have him dip a pencil eraser in blue paint, then press it onto the bag to resemble blueberries. While the students are decorating their blueberry buckets, ask an adult volunteer to hide blueberry snacks, such as blueberries in plastic bags that have been tied with blue ribbons, blueberry cereal bars, blueberry muffins, or blueberry tarts. When the paint dries, let the hunting begin! Have each child hold his blueberry bucket and his bear, and hunt for a blueberry snack. Enjoy another reading of *Blueberries For Sal* while your little ones snack, snack, snack!

Linda Ludlow
Bethesda Christian Schools
Brownsburg, IN

The Deep Blue Sea

Give your water table a feel of the deep blue sea with these exciting additions. Add several drops of blue food coloring to the water. Then add plastic or sponge undersea creatures such as sea horses, starfish, fish, jellyfish, crabs, and lobsters. Play a recording of ocean sounds while little ones dive into some serious play.

Dalia Behr—Preschool
The Little Dolphin School
Ozone Park, NY

Blue Jigglers®

Mixing up these colorful treats in your classroom will no doubt cure the blues. Prepare a pan of blue Jell-O® Jigglers® following the package directions. Then cut the gelatin into small squares to make individual Jigglers. Provide each child with several Jigglers on a blue paper plate; then allow your little ones to sample these yummy treats while listening to Sesame Street's Grover sing "I Am Blue."

Dalia Behr—Preschool

Blue-Jean Collage

It's all in the jeans—at least in this crafty collage. Provide each child with a blue construction-paper pant shape and scraps of old denim blue jeans. Have each student glue the denim scraps to the pant shape in the design of his choice. Now that's some casual creativity!

Theresa Anderson—Two- And Three-Year-Olds
Children's World Learning Center
Rochester, MN

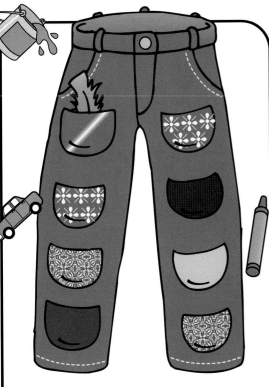

Pockets Full Of Blue

This fun-filled activity will be pockets full of fun. On a pair of old blue jeans, sew or hot-glue blue fabric to create pockets. Place a supply of different-colored small objects in a basket, making certain that there are enough blue objects for each pocket on the jeans. Place the jeans and the basket in a center. To use this center, a child chooses an object from the basket and identifies the color of the object. If the object is blue, he places it in one of the pockets on the pair of jeans. If the object is a different color, he places it back in the basket.

Deborah Ladd
Mustang, OK

I Spy Something Blue

All eyes are searching for something blue with this investigative idea. Provide each child with a cardboard tube that has been painted blue. Have each youngster hold his tube to his eye to represent a spyglass and look for blue objects around the classroom. Have a student volunteer name a blue object that he spies. Continue in this manner until each child has had a turn. Then take youngsters outside to search for other blue items. I spy a blue sky!

Kathy Mulvihill—Four-Year-Olds, Wee Care Preschool, Allendale, MI

A Blue Suncatcher

Put those old, blue crayons to good use by making colorful suncatchers. To make a suncatcher, grate various shades of blue crayons. Provide each child with two 3 1/2" squares of waxed paper. Have her sprinkle some of the crayon shavings on one piece of the waxed paper. Have her place the other waxed-paper square on top of the shavings. Place both sheets of paper on a towel; then place a cloth over the waxed paper. Gently press a warm iron atop the cloth until the crayon shavings in the center of the waxed paper have melted. When the paper has cooled, have each child glue four craft sticks over the edges of the paper square to make a frame. Glue a piece of blue yarn to the back to suspend the suncatcher. Now that's "blue-tiful"!

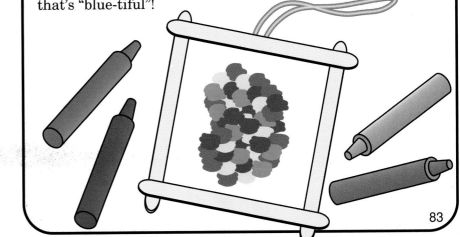

Get In Shape

Get your little ones into shapes with this well-rounded unit about circles.

ideas by Carrie Lacher

Buried Treasure

Set sail for an adventure on the high seas of learning with this discovery lesson about circles. To prepare for a class treasure hunt, gather a collection of round objects such as container lids, toy rings and bracelets, large buttons, juice-can lids, and poker chips. On the day of the hunt, hide the objects in your sand table. Place a supply of pails and scoopers nearby. Collect magazine pictures in which circular objects can be seen. Mount the pictures on construction paper and laminate the papers or place them in plastic page protectors. Display the pictures near the sand table. Or locate a copy of *Round & Round & Round* by Tana Hoban (check your library). On or near your sand table, place a sign that reads "Discover a treasure of circles!"

Gather your crew together and weave a tale of shipwrecked pirates. Describe to them a treasure that was buried on a forgotten island. Lead youngsters on a voyage through your classroom; then "land" at the sand table. Read aloud the sign that challenges them to discover circles. Carefully examine and discuss the displayed pictures or the pictures in *Round & Round & Round.* Then encourage them to dig into the sand to get a real feel for circles.

Circles All Around

Seat youngsters in a circle and ask them to brainstorm a list of items that are round. Write their suggestions on a large, bulletin-board-paper circle. As youngsters brainstorm, lead them to name food items that can be circular in shape such as snack crackers, LifeSavers®, CheeriOs®, pancakes, and orange or banana slices. Designate a day to be "Circle Day." Send a note home with each child asking him to bring a requested food item to school on that day. When the items arrive at school, arrange them on a round table that is covered with a round tablecloth. Provide each child with a paper plate; then encourage him to select the round items of his choice for snacking. The good-health reminder of the day? Don't forget to eat your circles!

Snacktime Shape-Up

Use these placemats at snacktime to help little ones define their space and to build shape-recognition skills. Personalize a large, white, construction-paper circle for each child. Provide youngsters with a supply of dot stickers and sponge-tipped dot markers for decorating the circles. Or make your own circular stamps by cutting circles from foam insoles. Mount the fabric side of each foam circle onto a sanded wood scrap. Encourage each child to press the stamps onto inkpads, then onto her paper circle.

When each child has decorated her placemat, ask her to describe her work. Write her comments on her mat; then laminate it or cover it with Con-Tact® covering to protect it from spills and crumbs. Read aloud the comments on a different placemat each day during snacktime.

Discover A Treasure Of Circles!

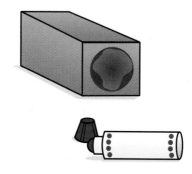

These circles are bubbles. They are flying.

Tabitha

With Circles

It's Circle Time!

Here's a riddle for your little ones. What do circles like best about preschool? Circle time—of course! Incorporate this movement activity into your group time and youngsters will soon be going around in circles. Using chalk draw a large circle on the floor of your group area; then cover the chalk outline with colorful tape. Invite the children to stand on the tape. Get those math muscles moving with this shapely song sung to the tune of "If You're Happy And You Know It." Create new verses by changing the movement from *tiptoe slowly* to *stomp your feet, slide sideways, hippity hop,* and more! Go ahead...act silly on the circle and go round!

A circle is a shape that goes round.
A circle is a shape that goes round.
A circle is a shape that goes round and
  round and round.
A circle is a shape that goes round.

[Tiptoe slowly] on the circle and go round.
[Tiptoe slowly] on the circle and go round.
[Tiptoe slowly] on the circle and go round
  and round and round.
[Tiptoe slowly] on the circle and go round.

Circle Prints

Get ready for squeals of delight when youngsters make this hands-on art project. Tape a large piece of bubble wrap (bubble side up) onto a flat surface. Invite a child to spread washable paint over the slippery, bumpy wrap. (Provide foam brushes for the sensorially squeamish.) Then have him quickly wash and dry his hands before pressing a large, construction-paper circle onto the wrap. Have him peel off the paper to reveal a collection of printed circles. When the prints are dry, provide magnifiers and display the prints where your circle explorers can examine up close the variations in the multitude of circles.

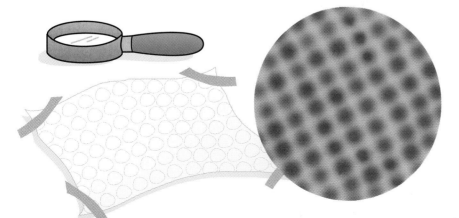

Going In Search Of Circles

Now that youngsters have experienced circles in a variety of ways indoors, it's time to take your circle search to the streets. Lead youngsters on a circle walk around your school, keeping a list as the students observe circles along the way.

Include families in on the fun by sending home a circular note suggesting that they conduct their own circle hunt.

Dear Parent, Go on a circle hunt! Help your child learn about circles by looking for circles at home.

Well-Rounded Reading

Circles, Triangles, And Squares
Written & Photographed by
Tana Hoban
(Out of print. Check your library.)

Ten Black Dots
Written & Illustrated by
Donald Crews
Published by Greenwillow Books

Wheel Away!
Written by Dayle Ann Dodds
Illustrated by Thacher Hurd
(Out of print. Check your library.)

Get In Shape

Teach youngsters about triangles with these fun activities that get right to the point.

ideas by Pamela Kay Priest

Triangle Town

Where's the best place to learn about triangles? Triangle Town, of course! In an open area of your room, establish the boundaries of Triangle Town by using colored tape to tape the outline of a large triangle onto the floor. Randomly tape smaller triangles inside the large triangle to create a maze of roads. Provide youngsters with various colors of construction-paper triangles, markers, glue, and cardboard tubes. Encourage them to create triangle trees and signs for Triangle Town. Supply triangular-shaped blocks and small cars for youngsters to play with while visiting the town.

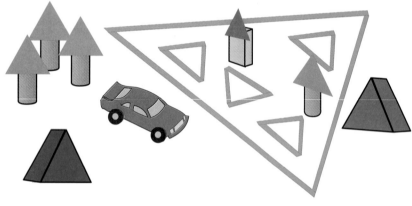

Musical Triangles

Accompany your triangle activities with the instrument of the day—the triangle. To make a triangle for each child, bend the hook of a hanger into a loop; then thread a four-inch length of yarn through the loop and tie it. Demonstrate how to hold the triangle by the yarn while tapping it lightly with a spoon. Give each child a triangle and spoon to play as children sing this triangle tune. Model how to keep a steady beat by tapping on the instrument. At the end of the song, tap each corner or side of the triangle as you sing, "One, two, three!"

Let's Bowl!

Youngsters will shape up their triceps as they set up triangles in this easy-to-make game of bowling. Locate an area suitable for bowling, such as a sidewalk, a hall, or an open area of your classroom. Set up ten cardboard tubes to form a triangle. Mark around the triangular tube arrangement with chalk. If the bowling lane will be indoors, tape over the chalk to indicate the area for the arrangement of the bowling tubes. If desired, also mark the spot where each tube should be placed to form the bowling arrangement. To play, a child rolls a soft ball toward the set-up tubes as if bowling. Encourage each child to count the tubes in the triangle arrangement when preparing for the next set. Thanksgiving is coming soon, so let's go for a *turkey*—three strikes in a row!

This Is A Triangle
(sung to the tune of "Row, Row, Row Your Boat")

This is a triangle.
Look and you will see.
It has three corners and three sides.
Count them. One, two, three!

With Triangles

Talking Turkey

This crafty turkey is a totally triangular dude! To make a turkey, each child will need a large, brown construction-paper triangle; a small, brown triangle; a supply of colorful construction-paper squares (including orange and red); glue; markers; and scissors. Glue the small, brown triangle to the larger triangle to represent the turkey's head and body. Cut the various colors of squares in half diagonally; then glue the resulting triangles to the back of the turkey's body in order to feather him. Cut an orange square in half diagonally; then glue each triangle to the base of the turkey to resemble legs. Color eyes; then glue small orange and red triangles to the tip of the turkey's head to create a beak and a wattle. So that the turkeys will be unique, provide each child with colored glue for embellishing the feathers of his turkey.

Two's Company, Three's A...Triangle!

Capture memories of your little ones getting into shape by creating this unique photo album. Place a large sheet of bulletin-board paper on the floor. Invite groups of three children at a time to lie on the paper and together form a triangle with their whole bodies, legs, arms, or fingers. Encourage each team to be creative. Take a picture of each group's pose. Glue each developed picture to a triangular-shaped piece of construction paper; then write the pictured students' names on the page. To make a photo album, title a cover "Triangles Of Friends"; then bind the pages together. Or display four, nine, or sixteen of the triangular-shaped pages together to form a giant triangle.

Jay, Brice, Justin

Triangle Problem Solving

The point of this center is to get youngsters' hands on triangles while developing their problem-solving skills as well. Store about 40 craft sticks in a container. As a group of children visits the center, demonstrate how to make a triangle using three sticks. Ask the children to help you count the sides and the corners of the triangle. Challenge the group to make as many triangles as they can or to make one giant triangle with the craft sticks. Encourage partners to make triangles with common sides. Before you know it, your little ones will have turned a corner on creative thinking.

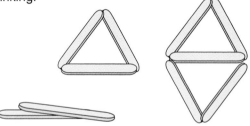

Eating To Stay In Shape

Eating to stay in shape is easy when the treats are triangles as well! Cut slices of bread, square sandwich meat, and cheese slices into triangles. If desired also provide condiments such as mayonnaise and mustard. Allow each child to make his own sandwich. On the side serve triangular-shaped chips and triangles cut from fruit rolls for dessert. Don't forget to provide square napkins folded into triangles. Why count calories when you can count corners? Shapely eating is as easy as one, two, three!

Get In Shape

Looking for shape fun? If so, then size up this unit. You're sure to find it's a square deal!

ideas contributed by Linda Rice Ludlow

Square Safari

In the jungle of your room are squares waiting to be discovered! To help your little ones spy squares, prepare "binocu-squares." To make a pair, cut off the end flaps from a margarine box. Draw a vertical line through the center of the back of the box and cut. Press the box flat so that the printed side is facing down. Fold one end of the box onto itself to meet the first crease; then fold again twice. Fold the opposite end in the same manner. Release; then refold each side to create rectangular tubes. Fold both tubes once again so that the sides touch in the center. Secure the tubes with tape. If desired, cover the completed pair of "binocu-squares" with paper.

Have each child look through a pair of the "binocu-squares" in search of unsuspecting squares around your room. At snacktime hide individual bags of square-shaped snacks such as crackers or sandwich quarters; then have youngsters search for the bags around the room. Everywhere, there's a square!

Celebrity Square

Make a square puppet to add personality to your focus on squares. Since your puppet is sure to be a celebrity, assist each child in making a square puppet of his own. To make a puppet, cut a construction-paper rectangle that measures exactly twice as long as it is wide. Fold the rectangle in half; then glue only the sides together. Encourage each child to use small paper squares and markers as desired to add facial features to his square. Teach youngsters the following song and encourage them to help their square puppets sing along!

Ode To A Square

(sung to the tune of "Clementine")

I have four sides
All the same size,
And my shape is called a square.
I can be so very useful,
And I'm seen 'most everywhere!

With Squares

The Mystery Of The Missing Square

Youngsters are sure to enjoy this shaped-up version of the game Doggy, Doggy, Who's Got Your Bone? To play, seat youngsters in a group. Ask a volunteer to sit in a chair with his back facing the group. Place a square cutout beneath the chair. Then silently motion for a child in the group to take the square, return to the group, and hide the square behind him. As a group chant, "[Child's name], [child's name], in the chair. Somebody came and took your square." The child in the chair then makes as many as four guesses (one for each side of the square) as to who took the square. Whether or not he guesses correctly, praise him for his effort and invite him to trade places with the child holding the square.

Gift-Wrapped Squares

Snacktime is all wrapped up with this special snack. Give each child a graham-cracker square to "wrap" by spreading it with frosting. If desired, have her decorate her package by adding candy sprinkles. To top the package with a bow, have her place a whole gumdrop on the center of the cracker, and then arrange four gumdrop halves around the whole gumdrop. This is one gift-wrapped package children won't have to wait to enjoy!

Squarely Centered

Get your blocks center all squared away with these suggestions. Remove all but the cube-shaped squares from your blocks center. Supplement the center with other cube-shaped items such as gift-wrapped boxes, square nesting cups, and plastic containers with lids. As each child builds, ask him to find the square sides of the blocks, boxes, containers, and lids in his structure.

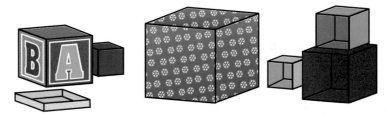

Be A Square!

You won't have to go on a square hunt to find youngsters who are willing to participate in this group activity. Divide your class into groups of four children each. Ask each child in a group to stand with her arms out; then show the children how to stand beside and in front of each other to form a group square. Then teach youngsters this shapely song.

We're A Square

(sung to the tune of "London Bridge")

Our four sides are just the same.
Just the same. Just the same.
Our four sides are just the same.
We're a square.

Get In Shape

Dazzle your youngsters as you use these sparkling activities to introduce the diamond shape.

ideas by Suzanne Moore

Presto "Change-o"

Amaze your little ones by introducing the diamond shape in this magical way. To prepare, spread glue onto the dull side of an 8" x 10" piece of foil. Press the foil onto a 9" x 12" piece of black construction paper. (Be sure the foil is completely attached to the paper so it does not separate during your magic act.) When the glue is dry, fold the paper in half so that the foil is inside. Using a pencil, lightly draw a five-inch-tall triangle on the black paper so that the base of the triangle is on the fold.

During a group time, keep the paper folded as you show your audience both sides. Review the attributes of a triangle as you dramatically cut it out of the paper. Holding the cutout at the top point, show the shape to the class. Then say the magic words, "Abracadabra, zim zam zimond. Turn this triangle into a diamond!" Flip the triangle open to reveal the diamond shape. If desired, follow up your trick by having students make their own magic diamonds in a similar manner.

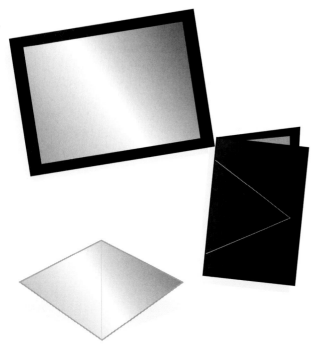

Let's Go Fly A Kite

Youngsters will be flying high—and getting a real feel for diamonds—when they make these fingerpainted kites. For each child, cut a used file folder into a diamond shape. Also cut two bow shapes from construction paper, and a length of crepe-paper streamer. Have the child place his shape on a cookie sheet or lunch tray; then provide him with various colors of fingerpaint. As he paints, help him describe the attributes of the diamond. Ask the child to set his kite aside to dry and to wash his hands. On one bow, write his description of where his kite would fly. Write his name on the second bow. Tape the bows to the streamer; then tape the streamer to the back of the kite. Suspend the kites from your ceiling. Look! Diamonds in the sky!

With Diamonds

Diamond Necklaces

These necklaces will polish off youngsters' abilities to recognize the diamond shape. For each child, cut a 5" x 3" diamond from tagboard, a 5" square from aluminum foil, and a 24" length of thick, glittery yarn. To make a necklace, wrap the foil around the shape. Punch a hole near the top of the shape; then thread the yarn through the hole. Tie the yarn at the top of the shape (so that it will lie flat when worn) and at the yarn ends. If desired, glue rhinestones to each of the four corners of the diamond. Diamond days are here again!

A Crown Of Diamonds

Your little kings and queens will feel like royalty when wearing these diamond-decorated crowns. Cut several tagboard diamond shapes and foil squares (as described in "Diamond Necklaces") for each child. Have each child cover each of her shapes with foil, then glue on craft jewels. Staple her decorated diamonds onto a sturdy sentence strip; then staple the ends of the strip so the crown fits on the child's head. Look! It's the duke and duchess of diamonds!

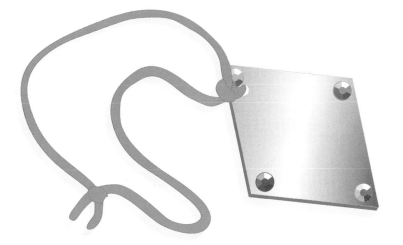

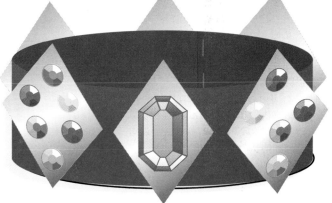

One Big Diamond

Follow up your kite craft (see "Let's Go Fly A Kite") by chanting this poem. If desired, draw a kite on a chalkboard. As you recite the poem, erase the tail of the kite to reveal a diamond.

One big diamond high in flight.
A diamond's shaped just like a kite.
Take away the tail, and what do I see?
A diamond looking back at me!

Home Run!

This movement idea is sure to be a hit! If your school has a baseball field, take youngsters out for a run around the giant diamond shape. Or arrange four game cones, game base markers, or placemats in an open area of your playground to indicate the four corners of a diamond. Have the class follow you as you run to each of the four corners of the diamond shape. Now that's a home run of an idea!

Diamond Jubilee

Diamonds are fun to wear but even more fun to eat! Invite your necklace- and crown-clad youngsters to visit a cooking center to prepare these delicious diamonds. To make one, cut a piece of bread into a diamond shape; then spread butter and jam onto the bread. Diamond desserts fit for royalty!

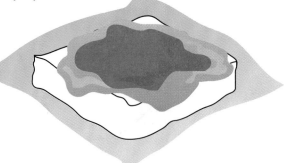

91

Get In Shape

Here it is! Our last set of exercises created to get your preschoolers into great shape! Use these activities to round out youngsters' knowledge of that oh-so-original oval.

ideas contributed by Barbara Meyers and Angie Kutzer

Looking For Ovals

Enlist the help of Little Oval to search for ovals in the classroom. To make the costume, cut a slit three-fourths of the way down both narrow sides of a paper grocery bag. Cut out an oval shape from tagboard, large enough to cover one of the wider sides of the bag; then glue it to the bag. Ask a child to put on the costume so that you can mark where to cut a smaller oval about the size of a child's face. Then cut the oval through both the bag and the larger oval. Label the costume "Little Oval."

Begin your oval unit by reading aloud *The Shape Of Things* by Dayle Ann Dodds (Candlewick Press). After reading, turn back to the page that focuses on ovals. Introduce the shape's name again and have youngsters trace imaginary ovals in the air. Invite a volunteer to put on the costume and become Little Oval. While the group quietly sings the following song, send him on a search to find an oval-shaped object in the classroom. Once the song ends, have Little Oval share his find.

Look What I Found!
(sung to the tune of "Five Little Ducks")

Oval shape went out one day
To find more oval shapes to play.
Oval shape looked all around,
Then with a smile said, "Look what I found!"

Little Oval

Optical Ovals

What can you do with potatoes, paint, and paper? Make oodles of oval prints! To get ready for the printing, slice several potatoes in half lengthwise; then fill several pie pans with different colors of tempera paint. Look again at the printed shapes in *The Shape Of Things*. Invite each student to dip a potato half into the paint and print several oval shapes onto a large sheet of art paper. When the paint is dry, encourage her to use markers and precut construction-paper shapes to turn her oval into a masterpiece. Display these creations along with the title "Can You Find The Ovals?" for others to ogle over.

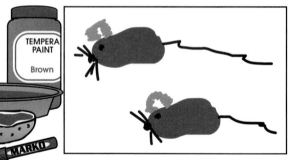

Oval Munchies

Your little ones are sure to be in great shape after making and munching on these "oval-wiches" at the cooking center. To make one, use an oval-shaped cookie cutter to cut an oval from two slices of bread and one slice of processed cheese. Place one oval of bread on an oval-shaped plate or a napkin cut into an oval shape; then add the oval of cheese. Squirt an oval of mustard or mayonnaise on top of the cheese before topping the sandwich with the second oval of bread. Lean to the left; lean to the right. Pick up your "oval-wich"; then take a bite!

With Ovals

The Oval Song

Use colored tape to make a large oval shape on the floor; then invite your little ones to hop, skip, march, and otherwise move around the tape while singing this catchy oval song.

I'm An Oval

(sung to the tune of "I'm A Little Teapot")

I'm an oval made with a curved line.
I think my egg shape looks mighty fine.
Eggs, potatoes, spoons, and race-tracks, too:
All have oval shapes just for you!

Get A Feel For It

Little fingers will do the walking with this tactile activity. Insert a variety of plastic or cardboard geometric shapes into a bag or box. (Make sure that there are more ovals than other shapes.) Challenge each child to reach into the bag and pull out an oval. Feeling for ovals is fun!

Stretch And Shape, Stretch And Shape

Cooperation is the key to this shapely exercise. To prepare, sew together the ends of a four-yard length of one-inch-wide elastic. Ask each child in a small group to hold onto the loop and work together to make an elastic oval shape. As a challenge, have the group stretch the loop into previously studied shapes, then back into an oval. What a workout!

Jelly-Bean Jamboree

End your shape training session with the best oval shapes of all—Jelly Belly® jelly beans! Fill a clear container with an assortment of the gourmet jelly beans. Seat your youngsters in an oval; then pass the container around the oval for each child to observe. List volunteers' descriptions about what they see. When the container returns to you, dispense a few jelly beans to each child. Encourage the students to touch, taste, and talk about the samples as you add to the descriptive list. (Be sure to use close supervision since jelly beans may be a choking hazard.) For added fun, request that your little ones try to guess the flavors of their jelly beans. Explain to your students that the candy company would like new jelly-bean designs and flavors. Give each child an oval-shaped paper platter, and invite him to use his choice of colorful paints and painting sponges to create his own jelly bean. As each child describes his jelly bean and names its flavor, ask the group to name the jelly bean's shape. Ovals, ovals, ovals!

Get In Shape

Are you ready for rectangles? Here's a rousing roundup of activities to help youngsters recognize rectangles.

by Angie Kutzer

Recognizing Rectangles

Gather a collection of empty food boxes with front panels that are rectangular in shape. Cut off the front panels; then show them to students during a group time. Ask volunteers to select panels and point out the long and short sides. Then encourage children to look for rectangular-shaped food boxes at home. Send a note to parents requesting that empty food boxes be sent to class. Set aside a few different-sized boxes for "Panel Printing" (below); then cut the front panels from the remaining boxes for use with the following activities.

Tall Or Short: Challenge volunteers to arrange the collection of rectangles so that they're all "standing tall"—so that the long sides are vertical—or "lying long"—so that the long sides are horizontal.

Rectangle Reading: To help little ones begin to recognize environmental print, display labels in a collage on a bulletin board or wall. Provide a pointer and encourage little ones to read the names of the foods or brands.

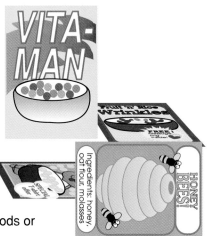

Panel Printing: Put your collection of uncut, empty food boxes in the art center. Pour several different colors of paint into separate shallow trays. Have a child dip the panel of a box into a tray. Then have him press the box onto a large sheet of construction paper. Encourage him to use different sizes of boxes and different colors to make his rectangular relic.

"Panel Printing" by
Diana Byrne—Pre-K
Harleysville, PA

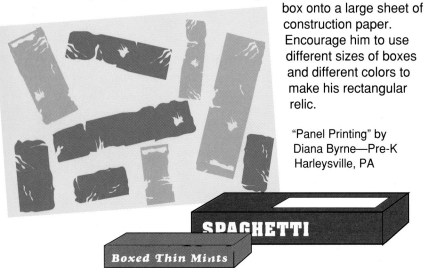

Romp And Rollick Round The Rectangle

Add a little rhythm and rhyme to your rectangle study. Using colored tape, make a large rectangle outline on your classroom floor. If desired, use one color of tape for the long sides and a different color for the short sides. Give each child a pair of building blocks or a set of sand blocks. Play excerpts from various slow and fast recordings. Encourage students to keep the beat with the blocks and their feet as they travel around the tape shape. For added fun, have them "freeze" every time the music stops. Look, we're doing the "rec-tango"!

Diana Byrne—Pre-K

Postcard Puzzlers

Get children's visual-discrimination and critical-thinking skills in shape with these rectangular puzzles. Gather an assortment of postcards. Cut each card into two or three pieces to make a postcard puzzle. Store each puzzle in a rectangular envelope. Or, for an added challenge, store the pieces to several cards in one envelope. Rectangles and postcards are a perfect fit!

With Rectangles

Rectangle Rodeo

Head out to the Rectangle Ranch to let your little broncobusters showcase their talents. Students will exercise their fine-motor skills and hand/eye coordination when making these rectangular horses *and* when bringing them back into the corral.

To make a horse, cut two 3" x 1 1/2" and one 6" x 3" white, black, brown, or tan rectangles from construction paper. Glue the rectangles together as shown. Cut lengths of yarn; then glue them to the horse to create a mane and tail. Glue one wiggle eye to each side of the horse's head. When the glue is dry, attach clothespins to the bottom of the rectangular body to represent the horse's legs. Personalize the horse; then slide a paper clip onto the horse's back.

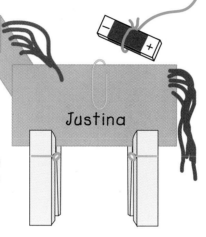

Justina

Place the horses in a basket or box (corral) along with a length of yarn tied around a magnet. During center time, stand the horses on the floor. Encourage a child to use the magnet to "lasso" each horse and put it back into the corral. Yippee-ki-yay!

Riddles On Rectangles

Collect a variety of objects that have a rectangular shape. (Refer to the following riddles for suggestions.) For each item, tell a riddle to help youngsters guess the identity of the object. Display the whole collection of items at all times. Once children are familiar with the objects, hide them in a box or bag. Pull out one at a time as guessed. What has two long and two short sides? A rectangle!

What Am I?

1. I am a rectangle. I can stand up or be hung on a wall. I decorate the edges of photographs. What am I? *(picture frame)*

2. I am a rectangle. I have lots of illustrations and words. I tell a story. What am I? *(book)*

3. I am a rectangle. I am sturdy and strong. The third little pig used me to build his house. What am I? *(brick)*

4. I am a rectangle—that is, until you chew me. I come in lots of different flavors. You can buy me in a little or big package. What am I? *(stick of gum)*

The Long And Short Of It

Help little ones differentiate between *squares* and *rectangles* with this catchy song. Hold up a rectangle and a square while singing the first verse, then just the rectangle during the second verse. Encourage the children to clap while singing the phrase "It's a rectangle," each time.

It's A Rectangle
(sung to the tune of "B-I-N-G-O")

There is a shape that has four sides,
But it is not a square….No!
It's a rectangle;
It's a rectangle;
It's a rectangle;
It is not like a square….No!

Two sides are long; two sides are short.
They all are not the same….No!
It's a rectangle;
It's a rectangle;
It's a rectangle;
The sides are not the same….No!

Cow Pattern
Use with "How Now, Purple Cow?" on page 79.

Crafts For Little Hands

Crafts For Little Hands

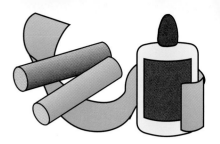

Apple Surprise

Leave youngsters starry-eyed when you cut several apples in half horizontally. Surprise! There are seedy stars inside! For a related art activity, pour green, red, yellow, and black tempera paint into separate pie tins. Cover a work area with newspaper. Personalize a white sheet of construction paper for each child. Provide each child an opportunity to dip an apple half into the red, yellow, or green paint, then press it onto his paper. After he has made several prints, instruct him to dip a finger in the black paint and then press it several times in the center of each apple print. When the paint is dry, display each set of prints or assist youngsters in cutting around the shape of each apple print. Laminate the cutouts if desired; then display them around a bulletin board for a delicious fall border.

Tammy Bruhn—Pre-K
Temperance, MI

Hand-Picked Apples

Fill separate pie pans with red and green washable tempera paint. Spread brown washable tempera paint in a shallow baking sheet. To create a design that resembles a tree trunk and limbs, ask a child to press his forearm and hand in the brown paint, then onto a personalized 12" x 18" sheet of blue construction paper. Assist the child in cleaning his arm. Next direct him to dip his thumb into the green paint and then press it onto the paper to resemble leaves on the tree. Direct him to dip a finger in the red paint, then onto the tree to resemble apples. When each child has printed a tree and the paint is dry, display the trees together in a row. That's quite an orchard you have there. It must be time to gather the harvest!

Sedona O'Hara—Preschool
University Children's School
California, PA

September Sunflowers

Perk up your classroom this September with the last sign of summer—sunflowers! To make a sunflower, cut a length of yellow crepe-paper streamer into one-inch-wide strips. Glue a set of strips along the edge of a two-inch brown construction-paper circle. Glue sunflower seeds to the opposite side of the brown circle. Cut out a green construction-paper stem and leaves. Glue the leaves to the stem and the stem to the base of the back of the flower. This crop of sunflowers is sure to make you smile.

adapted from an idea by Jan Hatch—Preschool
Jan's Preschool
Pleasant View, UT

Shiny Shakers

Add a little polish to craft time with these shiny apple shakers. To make a shaker, paint the backs of two small paper plates red. When the paint is dry, brush a mixture of two parts glue and one part water on the painted side of each plate to create a polished look. Allow the glue mixture to dry. Bend a brown pipe cleaner in half; then tape it to the rim of the unpainted side of one plate. Glue a green construction-paper leaf near the stem. Position the plates together so that the unpainted sides face each other. Staple the plates together, leaving an opening near the stem. Insert approximately ten dried beans in the opening; then staple the opening closed. Complete the shaker by squeezing a happy face on one side using a mixture of two teaspoons black powdered-tempera paint and four tablespoons white glue.

Melba Clendenin—Preschool, Chester Elementary School, Chester, IL

Pretty As A Peacock

The plumage on this pretty peacock is sure to please your preschoolers. To make a giant peacock, use large droppers to randomly drop yellow, blue, and purple tempera paints onto a piece of white bulletin-board paper. Dip a trim roller into a meat tray filled with green or blue paint; then roll it over the dots in an outward motion, creating a fan shape. When the paint is dry, complete the peacock by gluing a construction-paper body to the base of the painting as shown.

Pat Johnson—Three-Year-Olds
Church of the Redeemer
Columbus, OH

Beautiful Bovine

Your little ones will think this handsome holstein is simply "moo-velous." To make a cow, paint black spots on a large paper plate. Paint one small paper plate pink and another yellow. When the paint is dry, staple the pink plate near the bottom of the large plate to make a nose. Use a black marker to draw eyes, nostrils, and a mouth on the two plates. Cut the yellow plate in half; then trim the pieces to resemble horns. Staple the horns to the top back of the cow's head. Staple black construction-paper ears to the front of the plate; then bend them forward.

Pam Selby—Preschool: Developmentally Delayed, Walls Elementary, Walls, MS

Crafts For Little Hands

It Feels Like Fall

Give youngsters a feel for fall by encouraging them to feel and describe a real tree's trunk and freshly fallen leaves. As a follow-up, have little ones make artistic fall trees. Glue torn, brown construction-paper strips onto a large sheet of finger-painting paper to resemble the rough trunk and branches of a tree. Randomly drop spoonfuls of different colors of liquid tempera paint onto the paper. Cover the paper with a large sheet of waxed paper; then press and rub the paint. Allow the paint to dry completely; then peel away the waxed paper. Cut around the shape of the tree and its brightly colored, leaf-filled branches. Now it feels *and* looks like fall!

Bernadette Hoyer—Pre-K
Coles and McGinn Schools
Scotch Plains, NJ

Splat! It's A Spider!

Paint a child's palm and four fingers with black paint. Have her press her hand onto a sheet of construction paper twice so that the palm prints overlap and the finger prints extend in opposite directions. When the paint is dry, glue on colorful wiggle eyes. Even Miss Muffet would invite this spider to sit down beside her!

Kathy Folz
South Elementary
Franklin Park, IL

Feeling Spacey?

If you're feeling spacey, give this project a spin! Prepare a glittery mixture by combining one part glitter with two parts liquid starch. Paint the mixture onto celestial-shaped, construction-paper cutouts. When the shapes are dry, punch a hole in the top of each and thread with lengths of glittery yarn or thread. Tie the shapes onto a plastic hanger; then suspend the project from the ceiling. My stars! What a sight!

Lynne Bordeaux—Preschool
Miss Tanya's Nursery School
Westboro, MA

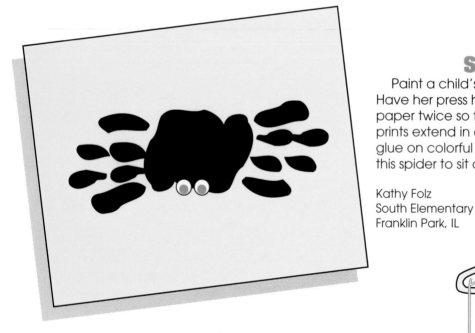

Plenty Of Pumpkin, Plenty Of Seeds!

That's what youngsters will find when you give them the opportunity to dig into a topless pumpkin. It's also what they'll find when they peek into this crafty pumpkin! From construction paper, cut a stem, a leaf, and two identically shaped pumpkins. Title one of the pumpkin cutouts "What's Inside A Pumpkin?"; then glue on the stem and leaf. To one side of the other pumpkin cutout, glue short pieces of orange yarn and real pumpkin seeds that have been washed and dried. Assemble the shapes with a brad as shown; then take a pumpkin peek!

Sonja M. Harrington—Pre-K
Tiny Tears Day Care
Albemarle, NC

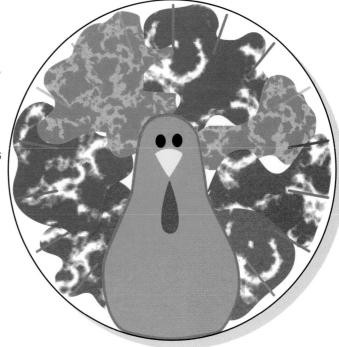

Turkey On A Platter

This turkey is already on a paper-plate platter and ready to serve as a Thanksgiving delight! Using different colors of tempera paint, sponge-paint a paper plate; then set the plate aside to dry. Using markers or crayons, decorate a pear-shaped, brown cutout to resemble a turkey's body. Glue the cutout to the plate. Better watch out! This turkey's so stunning he'll strut right off the table!

Gail Moody—Preschool
Atascadero Parent Education Preschool
Atascadero, CA

I am thankful for my new baby sister.

John

Wreath Of Thanks

Parents will be thankful for these decorative harvest wreaths and the sentiments written on them. To make a wreath, glue a construction-paper circle to the center of a paper plate. Glue crumpled squares of tissue paper around the rim of the plate; then glue a bow-shaped cutout to the bottom of the wreath. If desired, attach a small photo of each child to the bow on his wreath. In the center of the wreath, write the child's dictated sentence of thankfulness. To prepare the wreath for hanging, tape a length of ribbon to the back of the plate.

Debi Luke—Three- And Four-Year-Olds
Fairmount Nursery School
Syracuse, NY

Crafts For Little Hands

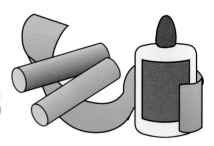

"Hand-y" Christmas Trees

Deck the halls with these terrific Christmas trees. To make a tree, press a hand into green tempera paint. Keeping the fingers and thumb close together, press the hand onto a sheet of white construction paper to represent tree leaves and branches. Cut a tree trunk from brown paper and glue it under the tree leaves. Then glue a gold or silver foil star to the top of the tree. To complete the project, use glitter glue, paint, or small candies to decorate the tree.

Tammy Bruhn—Pre-K, Ann Arbor, MI

Snowballs

Displaying these snowballs will create a spectacular winter sight. To make a snowball, place a Styrofoam® ball in the bottom part of an egg carton to prevent the ball from rolling. Brush the upper half of the ball with thinned white glue; then place white and blue tissue-paper squares on the glue. Brush glue on the tissue paper and add additional squares so that they overlap the others. Sprinkle silver or clear glitter sparingly over the wet surface. Allow the glue to dry and repeat the process to complete the other half of the ball. It's a snowball to keep!

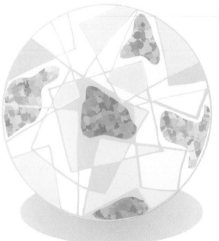

Wreath Ornaments

Spruce up any Christmas tree with these wreath ornaments. To make one, use green tempera paint to paint seven 2 1/2-inch-wide pieces of paper-towel or toilet-tissue cardboard tubes. When the paint is dry, thread a pipe cleaner through each of the pieces and twist the ends to secure it. Glue a red paper bow to the wreath. Thread a length of red ribbon through one of the cardboard pieces and suspend the wreath ornament on a tree for a festive display.

Martha Berry—Two-Year-Olds, Main Street Methodist Preschool
Kernersville, NC

Handy Menorah

Students' eyes will light up with excitement when they make these handsome menorahs. To make one, trace both hands onto a piece of yellow construction paper. Cut out the hand shapes; then glue them on a piece of blue construction paper so that the shapes of the pinkies overlap. Cut white paper flames; then glue a flame atop each of the candles. If desired, add glitter to the flames so they shine brightly throughout the season. Happy Hanukkah!

Lori J. Kracoff—Preschool
The Curious George Cottage Learning Center
Waterville Valley, NH

What An Angel!

Have each of your little angels make a look-alike cherub to give to her mom or dad. Cut an oval from the appropriate color of skin-toned construction paper. Glue the oval atop a gold or silver doily. Use markers to add facial features. Glue a handful of decorative moss to the top of the angel's head. Attach a metallic pipe-cleaner halo to the angel with a paper clip. Heavenly!

Sandra W. Scott—Pre-K
Asheville High Child Care
Asheville, NC

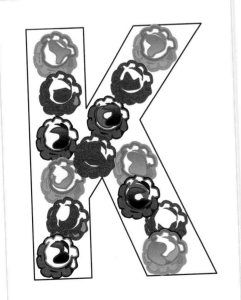

Corny Kwanzaa Craft

Here's a craft to help add meaning to your celebration of Kwanzaa. Break or cut an ear of corn into thirds. Prepare trays of red, black, and green tempera paint. Use the corn and paint to make creative prints on white construction paper. If desired, write a large *K* on a piece of paper. Print inside the outline of the letter with the corn. *K* is for Kwanzaa!

Dayle Timmons—Special Education Pre-K
Alimacani Elementary School
Jacksonville, FL

Crafts For Little Hands

"Thumb-ody" Loves You!

Loved ones will be touched by the message on these valentine gifts. To make a thumbprint hearts arrangement, cut various sizes of heart shapes from white or pink construction paper. Using red tempera paint, decorate the heart shapes with thumbprints. Set the hearts aside to dry. Personalize and write "Thumb-ody Loves You!" on a 4 1/2" x 8 1/2" piece of white paper. Tape the paper around a clean 12-ounce juice can. Glue a painted heart to the can; then glue the remaining hearts to craft sticks. Press a small amount of clay into the bottom of the decorated can; then tuck a section of red tissue paper into the can. Insert the sticks through the paper and into the clay. Isn't it nice to be reminded that "thumb-ody" loves you?

Martha Berry—Two-Year-Olds
Main Street Methodist Preschool
Kernersville, NC

Valentine Pockets

Looking for a creative way for youngsters to make their own valentine holders? Pick this pocket idea! Using pinking shears, cut off a third of a paper plate. Staple the larger cut plate to a full plate to make a pocket. Beginning at the top of the pocket, use a hole puncher to punch an even number of holes along the rims of the plates. Lace the plates together with a yard of red yarn. When you've finished lacing, tie the yarn into a loop at the top of the pocket. Decorate the pocket using paper heart cutouts and heart-shaped doilies. As a final touch, personalize the pocket and glue on a photo.

Elaine Dittman—Preschool
Holy Trinity Lutheran Preschool
Chicora, PA

Still Snowing?

If you love winter, you'll be delighted with these lovely snowflake wreaths. Prepare several snowflake templates to be used as stencils. (Or purchase decorative snowflakes from a party-suppy store.) To make a wreath, cut a large hexagon from white tagboard. Place a template on the tagboard; then sponge-paint the hexagon using pastel-colored paints. Arrange and press paper heart cutouts onto the wet paint. When the paint is dry, punch a hole through the top of the wreath; then tie on a length of yarn to make a loop. Invite parents to hang the wreaths on their doors as a winter welcome.

Brenda vonSeldeneck and Donna Selling—Four-Year-Olds
First Presbyterian Preschool
Waynesboro, VA

104

Shimmering Shamrocks

These shimmering shamrocks are sure to dazzle everyone who catches a glimpse of them. Have each child place a dab of blue and a dab of yellow finger paint atop a sheet of finger-paint paper. Then have him use his fingers to blend the colors together and paint the paper. While the paint is still wet, have each child sprinkle green glitter (and foil pieces if desired) atop the paint. When the paint dries, cut out a shamrock shape from each paper. These sparklers will add a festive touch to any classroom!

Tammy Bruhn—Pre-K
Temperance, MI

Love That Rainbow!

This cooperative art project will add a splash of color to your room. Using tape create arches on a half-round table to create separate sections of a rainbow. Then fill several pie pans with different colors of washable paint. Have your students finger-paint inside each arch with a different color of paint. When each arch has been painted, place a large sheet of white bulletin-board paper (slightly larger than the table) over the table. Gently press the paper onto the table. Carefully lift the paper; then let the paint dry. Trim the excess paper from around the rainbow. There you have it—a ravishing rainbow!

Joan Grossman
Bet Yeladim School
Columbia, MA

Suncatchers

Look out! These suncatchers are really hot! Tape a long sheet of clear Con-Tact® covering (sticky side up) onto a tabletop. Provide students with craft materials such as foil pieces, glitter, sequins, confetti, tissue paper, and shaped hole punchers. Have each child use the punchers to create shapes from various types of paper. Have each child choose from the items and sprinkle the selected ones atop the Con-Tact® covering, decorating as much of the covering as possible. Then place another sheet of clear Con-Tact® covering, identical in size and shape, atop the first sheet. Gently press the pieces together.

To display this cooperative project, suspend the sheet from a window for a sparkling presentation. To make individual suncatchers, cut out desired shapes from the decorated sheet of Con-Tact® covering. Punch a hole at the top of each suncatcher. Thread a length of ribbon or yarn through the hole; then suspend each suncatcher from a window.

Paula M. Piraino—Four-Year-Olds
Trinity Pre-School
Topsfield, MA

Crafts For Little Hands

Bunny Frame

You bet your whiskers! This frame should be given to "somebunny" special! To make one project, take a close-up picture of a child; then trim the developed photo into a circle. Mount the photo onto the center of a small paper plate. Glue white cotton balls around the photo. Glue pink cotton balls onto two poster-board bunny-ear shapes. Staple the ears to the top of the plate. Write an Easter message on a construction-paper bow-tie shape; then staple the tie to the front of the plate. If desired, attach a strip of self-adhesive magnetic tape to the back of the frame. Adorable!

Diane DiMarco—Preschool
Country Kids Preschool
Groton, MA

Handy Bunnies

Hippity, hoppity! This craft is sure to be a hands-down favorite! To make one bunny, paint a child's hand (excluding the thumb) white. Help the child separate her fingers into a V shape; then press her hand onto a sheet of construction paper. When the child's hand is clean and the paint is dry, direct the child to glue on wiggle eyes and a pom-pom nose. Next have her use markers to add whiskers and a smile. Have her also add pink paint to the bunny's ears. Finally, have the child twist the center of a tissue-paper rectangle, then glue it to the bunny to represent a bow tie.

Leigh Ann Clark—Four-Year-Olds
First Baptist Kindergarten, Eufaula, AL

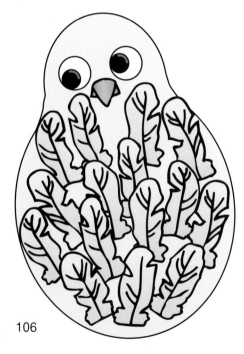

Look What Hatched!

Feathers will be flying in your classroom when youngsters make this fun craft project. To make one chick, trace a pear shape onto a large sheet of yellow construction paper. Next use an X-acto® knife to cut about 15 one-half-inch slits in the bottom part of the shape. Cut out the shape; then glue on wiggle eyes or paper eyes and a beak. Slide a yellow feather into each slot. (Feather dusters are a cheap source of feathers.) Turn the chick over; then tape each feather to the back. To really cause a hullabaloo, display these chicks together in a nest created by weaving together strips of brown paper.

Lisa Marie Bouldry—Four-Year-Olds
McLean Child Care Center
Belmont, MA

Fly, Butterfly!

These unique butterflies will grace your room with color. To make one butterfly, paint a paper plate as desired. Paint a cardboard tube black. When the paint is dry, cut the plate in half; then trim the straight sides as shown to resemble the outer edges of the wings. Glue the round edges to the tube. To complete the butterfly, tape two pipe cleaners in the top of the tube for antennae. To display these butterflies, hang them from your ceiling or near a window.

Michelle Pendley—Three-Year-Olds
The Children's Corner
Orange Park, FL

Winged Wonders

Wandering around in search of a simple and fun spring craft? These butterflies are wonderful for any of your preschoolers! Make a butterfly by using water-based markers to color two coffee filters. Spray the filters with water so that the colors blend. When the filters are dry, fold them in half. With the round edges together, slightly overlap the filters; then pinch them together in the center. Twist a pipe cleaner around the filters as shown. Curve the ends of the pipe cleaner to create the antennae. Surprise your little ones by using clear fishing line to dangle these butterflies in unusual places throughout your school or center.

Amy Jenkins—Preschool
Children's Country Day School
Mendota Heights, MN

Flannelboard Butterflies

Have your little ones make these beautiful butterflies; then use them on your flannelboard for counting practice and language activities. In advance, tint small amounts of water with food coloring. For each child, cut out a Pellon® butterfly shape; then use a permanent marker to add the child's initials. To add color to one shape, dampen it; then put it in a pie pan. Use an eyedropper to put small amounts of the tinted water onto the shape until no white is visible. Remove the shape from the pan to allow it to dry. Flannelboard fun takes flight with these beauties!

Kevin F. Humphrey—Head Start
Oxon Hill, MD

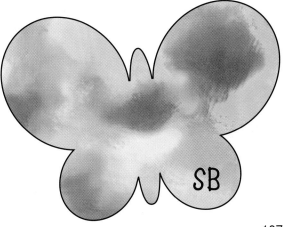

Flowers For A Special Lady

Each of your children can present a bouquet of long-lasting posies to his mom for Mother's Day. To make one bouquet, decorate a paper lunch bag with any of a variety of art materials, such as crayons, paint, flower stickers, flower stamps, or cut-out magazine pictures of flowers. Open the bag; then fold the top of the bag down about one inch. After putting the stems of several artificial flowers in the bag, squeeze the bag together just below the fold. Secure the flowers in the bag by tying a length of ribbon around the top of the bag. Flowers—for you!

Margaret Watts
15th Street Church Of God
Centralia, IL

An Expression Of Love

The love that fills this Mother's Day greeting keeps growing and growing and growing! To make one card, fold a sheet of construction paper in half. Write the message shown on the front and inside of the card. To decorate the front, glue on groups of scrunched tissue-paper squares to resemble flowers; then use a marker to add stems. As a special surprise, tape a package of marigold seeds to the inside of the card. If desired, send along planting instructions with a suggestion that mother and child spend some quality time together planting the seeds.

Debi Luke—Preschool
Fairmount Nursery School
Syracuse, NY

My love for you...

...grows and grows and grows!

MARIGOLD SEEDS

Happy Mother's Day!
Love, Stephen

My mom is "berry" special! Here's why!

My mom looks very pretty when she brushes her hair.

My mom's favorite thing to do is talk on the phone.

I love my mom because she sings to me.

Shelly

"Berry" Special Card

Here's a "berry" special card for a very special mom! Fold a large sheet of construction paper in half. To decorate the outside of the card, paint one side of a plastic berry basket green. Press the basket on the card to leave a print. Next sponge-paint red heart shapes above the basket to resemble strawberries. Dip a toothpick in white or black paint to add seeds to the berries. Finally, use a small piece of sponge to paint green leaves on the berries. To complete the inside of the card, write the message shown on the top of a white page. Ask a child to complete several sentence starters such as those shown. Record his answers. When the paint on the front of the card is dry, glue the page to the inside of the card.

Cheryl Cicioni—Preschool
Kindernook Preschool
Lancaster, PA

108

Crafts For Little Hands

We're Talkin' Turtles!

Don't be a slowpoke to try out this turtle craft! To get started, collect soft cardboard produce separators found in boxes of apples at your local grocer. Cut the cardboard apart so that you have a class supply of shapes to serve as turtle shells. To make one turtle, use tempera paint to paint a shell green or brown. From construction paper, cut out four turtle legs, a head, and a tail; then glue the shapes to the underside of the dry shell. Use markers and wiggle eyes to add details to the legs and head. Display the projects on a bulletin-board-paper pond along with rocks and a collection of Franklin books by Paulette Bourgeois.

Barbara Meyers
Fort Worth Country Day
Fort Worth, TX

Dazzling Dragonflies

Dazzle 'em with these easy-to-make dragonflies! To make one, use markers to add eyes and some color to an old-fashioned wooden clothespin. Next tie a ten-inch length of monofilament line into a loop. Also cut two rectangles (about 5" x 8") from different colors of cellophane. Holding the clothespin with the open end up, slide the loop, then the two cellophane pieces into the clothespin. Dangle these dainty insects in front of a sunny window.

Sharon M. Coulter
Park Place Children's Center
Muncie, IN

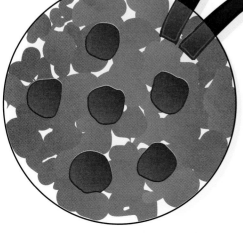

Pretty Polka-Dotted Ladies

Youngsters will scurry over to make one of these ladybugs. To make one, cut a pair of same-sized circles from waxed paper. Place one of the circles, waxed side up, on a newspaper-covered surface. Sprinkle red crayon shavings over the circle; then add black construction-paper circles and antennae. Place the remaining circle on top of the first. Cover the layers with a second piece of newspaper; then use an iron (on a low heat setting) to melt the wax. Are you seeing spots yet?

Kimberli Carrier—Preschool
Wise Owl Preschool
Nashua, NH

Flashy Fish

Splish, splash! These flashy fish will swim by just in time to create a fantastic display. To create a one-of-a-kind fish, glue oval-shaped tissue paper and foil pieces onto a white construction-paper fish shape. Attach a black dot sticker to resemble an eye. Punch a hole near the mouth of the fish. To display, suspend a length of rope from your ceiling; then attach the fish to the rope by sliding one end of an opened paper clip through the rope and the other end through the fish's mouth. Wow—what a catch!

Gail Moody—Preschool
Atascadero Parent Education Preschool
Atascadero, CA

Handprint Octopus

Journey to the depths of the ocean and you'll find these awesome octopi. Using fluorescent, liquid tempera paint, paint a child's palm one color and his fingers (excluding his thumb) four different colors. With his hand slightly tilted to one side, have him press his hand on a sheet of black construction paper. Then have him press just his fingers under the palm print to resemble the remaining four arms of the octopus. When the paint is dry, glue two wiggle eyes to the octopus and add facial features with a marker. If desired add ocean-related stickers to the paper to create an underwater scene.

Jan Stremel—Four-Year-Olds
St. Paul Preschool
Dallas, TX

Sweet Starfish

Students will create star-quality starfish with this sweet painting technique. Combine sugar and several drops of food coloring with enough water to create a thick but paintable mixture. Use crayons to add features to a construction-paper starfish. Then paint the sugar mixture onto the starfish or spread the mixture on with your fingers. When the sugar mixture is dry, add these sweet starfish to a sand-and-surf display.

Joannie Netzler—Three-Year-Olds
A Special Place
San Jose, CA

SONGS & SUCH

School Song

(sung to the tune of "Polly Wolly Doodle All The Day")

Oh, I go to school to learn and play,
Singing polly wolly doodle all the day!
Oh, I go to school to learn and play,
Singing polly wolly doodle all the day!

Fare thee well. Fare thee well.
Fare thee well, dear Mom (Dad) today!
For I go to school to learn and play,
Singing polly wolly doodle all the day!

Betty Silkunas • Lansdale, PA

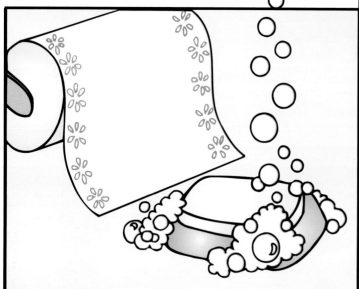

Singing As They Scrub

To encourage little ones to thoroughly wash their hands—rather than just give them a quick rinse—teach your children the following song. Then ask that each child sing the song through twice while he washes his hands.

(sung to the tune of "Clap, Clap, Clap Your Hands")

Wash, wash, wash your hands.
Play this cleanup game.
Rub. Scrub. Scrub and rub.
Germs go down the drain.

Donna Leonard—Preschool • Head Start • Dyersville, IA

The Apple Tree

While singing the first stanza of this song, have students walk in a circle, holding hands. During the second stanza, have the children stop and pretend to climb a tree. During the third stanza, encourage them to pretend to pick apples from a tree.

(sung to the tune of "Here We Go 'Round The Mulberry Bush")

Here we go 'round the apple tree, the apple tree, the apple tree.
Here we go 'round the apple tree on a cool and sunny morning.

This is the way we climb the tree, climb the tree, climb the tree.
This is the way we climb the tree on a cool and sunny morning.

This is the way we pick the fruit, pick the fruit, pick the fruit.
This is the way we pick the fruit on a cool and sunny morning!

Deborah Garmon—Preschool & Daycare
Pooh Corner Preschool And Daycare • Old Mystic, CT

Leaving The Sand Outside

Want youngsters to leave most of the sand outside in the sandbox? Sing and act out this song with your little sand lovers to ensure that most of the grit stays where it belongs.

(sung to the tune of "Row, Row, Row Your Boat")

Clap, clap, clap your hands.
Clap the sand away.
Clap, clap, clap your hands.
Clap the sand away.

Brush, brush, brush your arms (legs).
Brush the sand away.
Brush, brush, brush your arms (legs).
Brush the sand away.

Stomp, stomp, stomp your feet.
Stomp the sand away.
Stomp, stomp, stomp your feet.
Stomp the sand away.

Shake, shake, shake yourself.
Shake the sand away.
Shake, shake, shake yourself.
Shake the sand away. Hey!

Debbie Berthold—3-year-olds • Emmanuel Day School • Virginia Beach, VA

Car Wash

Turn your waterplay table into a car wash for the day. Include sponges, gentle liquid cleanser, and a few toy cars. To give your car wash a musical lift, teach youngsters the song that follows:

(sung to the tune of
"The Oscar Mayer® Weiner Theme Song")

Oh, I really like to give a car a car wash.
Squirting, soaping, scrubbing dirt away!
Oh, I really like to give a car a car wash.
Why, I could sing and scrub away the day!

Betty Silkunas • Lansdale, PA

SONGS & SUCH

Autumn Is Here

Have each child tape die-cut leaves to a length of yarn or clear fishing line. Then invite him to whirl and swirl his leaves while singing this autumn song.

(sung to the tune of "Have You Ever Seen A Lassie?")

The leaves are really changing,
And changing, and changing.
The leaves are really changing,
For autumn is here.

See red leaves and brown leaves,
And green leaves and gold leaves.
The leaves are really changing,
For autumn is here!

Linda Rice Ludlow—Preschool, Bethesda Christian School
Brownsburg, IN

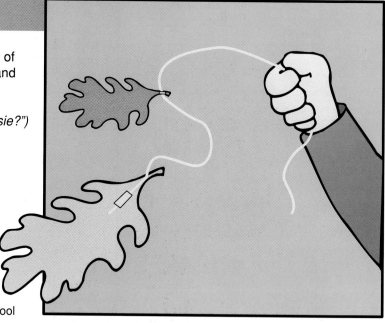

Halloween Pretending

Each time you sing this song, invite a student to pretend to be the character of her choice. Pretending is fun!

(sung to the tune of "Clementine")

Halloween is such a fun time.
It's not scary, not for me.
I pretend I'm someone different.
It's as fun as fun can be.

Mary Sutula, Orlando, FL

Mr. Scarecrow

(sung to the tune of "Twinkle, Twinkle, Little Star")

Mr. Scarecrow standing tall,   *(Hold hand above head and look up.)*
You just don't scare me at all.   *(Shake head "no.")*
Stuffed with straw from head to toe.   *(Touch head; then touch toes.)*
Quite a funny guy to know.   *(Hold tummy and chuckle.)*
Mr. Scarecrow standing tall,   *(Hold hand above head and look up.)*
You just don't scare me at all!   *(Shake head "no.")*

Betty Silkunas
Lansdale, PA

Falling Leaves

This smooth, soft autumn song gives little ones practice with slow and controlled movement. Before adding motions to the song, discuss the movement of leaves and how leaves might be affected by the wind. As a music extension, use a set of bells or an Autoharp® to help children hear the downward movement of the melody. Encourage them to show this downward movement with their bodies as they dance freely to the song.

Leaves are fal-ling down.
Slow-ly to the ground.
Some are gold. Some are brown.
Nev-er make a sound.

Dr. Grace Morris • Southwest Texas State University • San Marcos, TX

Leaves Are Falling Down

Leaves are fal-ling down.
Slow-ly to the ground.
Some are gold. Some are brown.
Nev-er make a sound.

The Pumpkins Are Here

After introducing the song, give each youngster a pumpkin cutout that has been mounted on a straw or a craft stick. As the song is sung, have each youngster hold his pumpkin as indicated by the words.

(sung to the tune of "The Farmer in The Dell")

The pumpkins are here; the pumpkins are there.
The pumpkins, the pumpkins are everywhere.

The pumpkins are up; the pumpkins are down.
The pumpkins, the pumpkins are all around.

The pumpkins are in; the pumpkins are out.
The pumpkins, the pumpkins are all about.

The pumpkins are low; the pumpkins are high.
The pumpkins, the pumpkins all say, "Good-bye."

Lucia Kemp Henry

Gobbly, Wobbly Turkeys

(sung to the tune of "Ten Little Indians")

One little, two little, three little turkeys,
Gobbly, wobbly, bobbly turkeys,
Hurry, scurry, worry turkeys,
It's Thanksgiving Day!

Betty Silkunas • Lansdale, PA

SONGS & SUCH

Ten Little Latkes

(sung to the tune of "Pawpaw Patch")

One little, two little, three little latkes;
Four little, five little, six little latkes;
Seven little, eight little, nine little latkes;
Ten little latkes for a Hanukkah treat!

We peeled and chopped and grated our potatoes.
Peeled and chopped and grated our potatoes.
We peeled and chopped and grated our potatoes.
Ten little latkes for a Hanukkah treat!

We put them in the pan and fried them in the oil.
Put them in the pan and fried them in the oil.
We put them in the pan and fried them in the oil.
Ten little latkes for a Hanukkah treat!

They fried and sizzled until they were brown.
Fried and sizzled until they were brown.
They fried and sizzled until they were brown.
Ten little latkes for a Hanukkah treat!

We smelled them, ate them—mmm…how delicious!
Smelled them, ate them—mmm…how delicious!
We smelled them, ate them—mmm…how delicious!
No more latkes for a Hanukkah treat!

Kathy Cotton—Preschool
Stepping Stones Preschool, Westport, CT

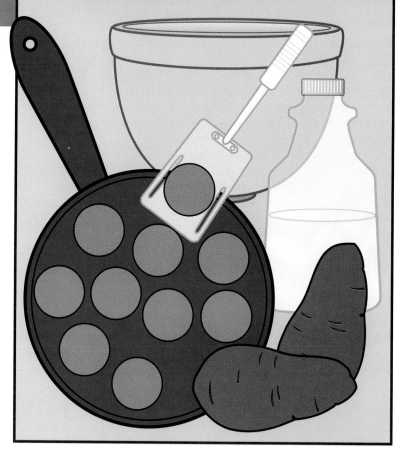

Little Pine Tree

(sung to the tune of "Clementine")

Little pine tree, little pine tree,
You have branches green and wide. *Stretch arms out to sides.*
Little pine tree, little pine tree,
Gently sway from side to side. *Sway body from side to side.*

Little pine tree, little pine tree,
In the winter woods you grow. *Hold arms above head.*
Little pine tree, little pine tree,
Stand so bravely in the snow. *Stand on tiptoes; stretch arms up.*

Little pine tree, little pine tree,
You have snowflakes in your hair! *Wiggle fingers above head.*
Little pine tree, little pine tree,
Welcome birds to shelter there. *Make a welcoming motion.*

Lucia Kemp Henry

An Instrumental Snowstorm

Explore the concepts of loud, soft, fast, and slow with this blizzard of an idea. You will need instruments that make ringing sounds such as bells, finger cymbals, and triangles, as well as instruments that make swishing sounds such as sand blocks and shakers. Give each child an instrument. After providing an opportunity for free exploration of the instruments, help the children separate into groups based on instruments that sound alike. Create a snowstorm by having the children begin to play their instruments slowly and softly. To create the effect of a building snowstorm, encourage the children to gradually play faster and louder. As the snowstorm peaks, direct children to begin playing slowly and softly again. Whew! What a storm!

Dr. Grace Morris, Southwest Texas State University, San Marcos, TX

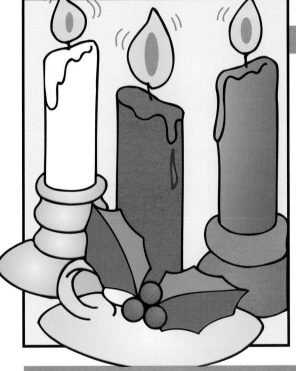

Here's A Little Candle

Many winter holidays share the hope for love and warmth symbolized by light. Whether your little ones will light a Christmas candle, a menorah, or a candle to celebrate Kwanzaa, this is a holiday song that everyone can sing together.

(sung to the tune of "I'm A Little Teapot")

Here's a little candle dressed in white,
Wearing a hat of yellow light.
When the night is dark, then you will see
Just how bright this light can be!

Here's a little candle straight and tall,
Shining its light upon us all.
When the night is dark, then you will see
Just how bright this light can be!

Here's a little candle burning bright,
Keeping us safe all through the night.
When the night is dark, then you will see
Just how bright this light can be!

Lucia Kemp Henry

Friends

Join hands for peace and sing this song to celebrate the birthday of Dr. Martin Luther King, Jr.

(sung to the tune of "Jingle Bells")

Friends hold hands. Friends hold hands.
Friends hold hands and smile.
All our classmates are our friends.
Let's sing with them awhile.

(Repeat verse.)

Betty Silkunas

SONGS & SUCH

I'll Send You A Letter

If you're looking for a way to practice name recognition, this first-class game really delivers! Personalize an envelope for every child. If desired, tuck a small treat—such as a valentine or stickers—inside each envelope. Also locate a real or dramatic-play mailbox near your group area. To begin, hand an envelope to a child in the group. Instruct her to put the envelope in the mailbox as the group sings the first and second verses of the following song. Appoint a volunteer postal worker to remove the envelope from the box, and to deliver it to the appropriate child as the group sings the third verse. Continue until each child has delivered and received a letter.

(sung to the tune of "For He's A Jolly Good Fellow")

I'll send you a letter.
I'll send you a letter.
I'll send you a letter.
This letter is to [Child's name].

I'll put it in the mailbox.
I'll put it in the mailbox.
I'll put it in the mailbox.
This letter is to [Child's name].

I'll bring you a letter.
I'll bring you a letter.
I'll bring you a letter.
This letter is to [Child's name].

adapted from a song by D. Lyn Stevens—Preschool
A.M. Chaffee School
Oxford, MA

It's Shadow Time!

(sung to the tune of "The Itsy-Bitsy Spider")

The furry, little groundhog
Goes in his hole to sleep;
Through the cold winter's
Snow and ice so deep.

In February,
He stretches to and fro.
Does the furry, little groundhog
Get scared by his shadow?

Funny Valentine

(sung to the tune of "Did You Ever See A Lassie?")

Here's a funny little valentine, a valentine, a valentine,
A happy little heart with a message for you.
It says something special. I bet you can guess it.
My funny little valentine says, "I love you!"

Cheryl Cicioni—Preschool
Kindernook Preschool
Lancaster, PA

Be My Valentine

(sung to the tune of "Clementine")

Won't you be my valentine,
Be my valentine today?
For you are my special friend.
Be my valentine today!

Linda Rice Ludlow—Preschool
Bethesda Christian Schools
Brownsburg, IN

Brush, Brush, Brush Your Teeth

(sung to the tune of "Row, Row, Row Your Boat")

Brush, brush, brush your teeth,
Every night and day.
That's the way to healthy teeth.
Keep cavities away!

Pretend to brush teeth.
Head on hands to "sleep"; then "wake up."
Point to teeth.
Hand out in front to say, "Stop."

Brush, brush, brush your teeth,
Up and down each day.
See your dentist twice a year.
Keep cavities away!

Pretend to brush teeth.
Stretch up; then bend down.
Show two fingers.
Hand out in front to say, "Stop."

Linda Rice Ludlow—Preschool

SONGS & SUCH

When Spring Comes Rolling In

(sung to the tune of "When The Saints Go Marching In")

Oh, when spring
Comes rolling in,
Oh, when spring comes rolling in,
[The flowers will all start blooming]
When spring comes rolling in.

Repeat, substituting the phrases below for the underlined words.

The plants will all start growing...

The birds will all start nesting...

The bees will all start buzzing...

LeeAnn Collins—Director, Sunshine House Preschool
Lansing, MI

Bug Song

(sung to the tune of "If You're Happy And You Know It")

Oh, I wish I were an eensy-weensy spider.
Yes, I wish I were an eensy-weensy spider.
I'd go "creepy-creepy-crawly" down your hall and up your "wall-y"!
Oh, I wish I were an eensy-weensy spider.

Oh, I wish I were a yellow honeybee.
Yes, I wish I were a yellow honeybee.
I'd go "buzzy-buzzy-buzzy" and my stripes would be all fuzzy!
Oh, I wish I were a yellow honeybee.

Oh, I wish I were a wiggly caterpillar.
Yes, I wish I were a wiggly caterpillar.
I'd go "munchy-munchy-munchy." All the leaves would be my "lunch-y"!
Oh, I wish I were a wiggly caterpillar.

Oh, I wish I were a small red army ant.
Yes, I wish I were a small red army ant.
I'd go "trompy-trompy-trompy" over hills and through the "swamp-y"!
Oh, I wish I were a small red army ant.

Oh, I wish I were a hungry little skeeter.
Yes, I wish I were a hungry little skeeter.
I'd go "bitey-bitey-bitey" when you went outside at "night-y"!
Oh, I wish I were a hungry little skeeter.

Vicki Widman—Pre-K, A.J. Stepansky Early Childhood Center
Waterford, MI

In The Farmyard

Animal noises abound in this lively tune! Have your young farmhands sing it several times, substituting other animals and animal noises for the underlined words.

(sung to the tune of "My Bonnie Lies Over The Ocean")

The [cow] lives out in the farmyard.
She's an animal I go to see.
The [cow] lives out in the farmyard
And sometimes she says things to me.
["Moo, moo, moo, moo."]
That's what the [cow] says to me, to me.
["Moo, moo, moo, moo."]
That's what the [cow] says to me!

adapted from a song by LeeAnn Collins—Director
Sunshine House Preschool, Lansing, MI

Flitter, Flutter, Butterfly

Invite youngsters to make fluttering finger puppets to accompany this song. To make a puppet, cut a simple butterfly shape from construction paper. Attach a strip of wide masking tape to the center of one side of the cutout. Then fold the cutout in half and cut two slits, about 3/4" apart, through both the paper and the tape. Unfold the cutout. A child may slip one or two fingers through the slits to operate the puppet.

(sung to the tune of "Twinkle, Twinkle, Little Star")

Flitter, flutter, butterfly,
Flying in the big blue sky.
Flutter high and flutter low.
Flutter fast and flutter slow.
Flitter, flutter, butterfly,
Flying in the big blue sky.

puppet idea by Diane White—Preschool, Rotary Youth Centre Preschool Program
City Of Burlington, Burlington, Ontario, Canada

The Itsy-Bitsy Seed

Teach little ones the accompanying motions to this tune. It'll grow on you!

(sung to the tune of "The Itsy-Bitsy Spider")

The itsy-bitsy seed was planted in a hole.	*(Pretend to plant seed in palm.)*
Down came the rain and a sprout began to grow.	*(Wiggle fingers downward.)*
Out came the sun and shone down on the leaves.	*(Place arms in circle overhead.)*
Now the itsy-bitsy seed is a great big grown-up tree!	*(Raise hands above head, fingers spread wide.)*

Kimberly Boston—Preschool, Brooklyn Blue Feather Early Learning Center, Brooklyn, NY

In The Zoo

(sung to the tune of "The Farmer In The Dell")

The monkeys in the zoo,
The monkeys in the zoo,
They bend their knees and swing from trees,
The monkeys in the zoo.

The zebras in the zoo,
The zebras in the zoo,
They look so right in black and white,
The zebras in the zoo.

The seals in the zoo,
The seals in the zoo,
They swim and splash the whole day through,
The seals in the zoo.

The lions in the zoo,
The lions in the zoo,
They lift their heads and give a roar,
The lions in the zoo.

The children at the zoo,
The children at the zoo,
They have such fun till the day is done,
The children at the zoo.

Elizabeth McDonald—Preschool, School Readiness Center
Naperville, IL

Camping Trip

Have any of your little ones ever been camping? Have them tell about their adventures. Better yet, invite a parent to bring camping supplies—such as a sleeping bag, backpack, and flashlight—to your class. Include each item discussed below.

(sung to the tune of "Brush Your Teeth" as sung by Raffi)

We're going on a camping trip, and what will we bring?
We're going on a camping trip, and what will we bring?
We'll bring a [tent]. (Clap, clap, clap, clap, clap, clap, clap, clap, clap.)
We'll bring a [tent]. (Clap, clap, clap, clap, clap, clap, clap, clap, clap.)

Dianna Bruckner—Two-Year-Olds, Winter Park Day Nursery
Winter Park, FL

"Dino Ditty, Ditty Dum Ditty Do"

Here's a song that's a real blast from the past!

(sung to the tune of "Do Wah Diddy Diddy")

Here he comes just a stomping with his feet,	*Stomp.*
Singing "dino ditty, ditty dum ditty do."	*Clap.*
Searching all around for something good to eat,	*Hand over brow.*
Singing "dino ditty, ditty dum ditty do."	*Clap.*
He's huge. (He's huge.) He's strong. (He's strong.)	*Stretch out arms; then bend elbows and make fists.*
He's huge, he's strong, won't be hungry very long.	*Repeat arm motions; then shake finger "no."*
"Dino ditty, ditty dum ditty do…"	*Clap.*
"Dino ditty, ditty dum ditty do…"	*Clap.*

Marsha Feffer—Four-Year-Olds, Salem Early Childhood Center/Bentley School
Salem, MA

We're On Our Way!

(sung to the tune of "Down On Grandpa's Farm")

We're on our way, we're on our way, on our way to kindergarten.
We're on our way, we're on our way, on our way to kindergarten.

Over in kindergarten, we will learn new things.
Over in kindergarten, we will learn new things.
In kindergarten, we'll learn to say and write our ABCs!
In kindergarten, we'll learn to say and write our ABCs!

We're on our way, we're on our way, on our way to kindergarten.
We're on our way, we're on our way, on our way to kindergarten.

Over in kindergarten, we will make new friends.
Over in kindergarten, we will make new friends.
With our friends, we will play new games. Yippee!
With our friends, we will play new games. Yippee! Oh…

We're on our way, we're on our way, on our way to
    kindergarten.
We're on our way, we're on our way, on our way to
    kindergarten.

Roberta Bryce—Four-Year-Olds, Our Lady Of The Angelus School
Rego Park, NY

Summertime Song

Summertime is a fun time! Ask youngsters to name things they like to do in the summer, such as swim, run, and ride. Then include their ideas in this summertime song.

(sung to the tune of "Mary Had A Little Lamb")

Summer is the time to [play],
Time to [play], time to [play].
Summer is the time to [play].
Enjoy those sunny days!

Lucia Kemp Henry

Splashing's So Much Fun!

Heading to the pool, lake, or ocean for a swim? Have a splashing good time!

(sung to the tune of "Ten Little Indians")

One big, two big, three big splashes,   *Sing loudly.*
Soaking even my eyelashes!
I like making water smashes;
Splashing's so much fun!

One little, two little, three little splashes,   *Sing softly.*
Soaking even my eyelashes!
I like making water smashes;
Splashing's so much fun!

Betty Silkunas, Lansdale, PA

Did You Ever See A Fishy?

Did you ever see a fishy move left and right? How about front and back, or up and down? Designate a pair of movements each time you sing this song. Then encourage your school of fish to swim this way and that.

(sung to the tune of "Did You Ever See A Lassie?")

Did you ever see a fishy, a fishy, a fishy,
Did you ever see a fishy swim this way and that?
Swim this way and that way, and that way and this way?
Did you ever see a fishy, swim this way and that?

IT'S CIRCLE TIME!

Circle-Time Song

Invite youngsters to join you in singing this circle-time song to the tune of "This Old Man."

Circle time, circle time—
It's a very special time!
Let's go to the carpet
And we'll have some fun!
Circle time's for everyone!

Janis Woods—Four-Year-Olds, Ridgeland Elementary, Ridgeland, SC

Honey Hunt

For a "beary" special snack and activity that every child is sure to enjoy, have a honey hunt! For each child, prepare a honey pot by gluing yellow construction-paper honey to a paper lunch bag. Label each bag "Honey Pot." Prepare a bear headband for each child by gluing brown, construction-paper semicircles to the top of a stapled sentence strip. As a final preparation, partially fill a zippered plastic bag with Honeycomb® cereal for each child. Hide the bags around the classroom when the children are not present.

Then, during circle time, invite youngsters to put on their bear headbands, pick up their honey pots, and forage for honey! As each child locates a plastic bag of cereal, encourage him to place it in his honey pot and return to the circle area. Then invite your hunters to eat their cereal snacks. Mmmm...I'm as hungry as a bear!

Linda Rice Ludlow—Four-Year-Olds, Bethesda Christian School, Brownsburg, IN

Sign Language

Help young children practice their budding communication and fine-motor skills when you teach them sign language as part of your circle-time routine. (If you're not familiar with sign language, check out a book from your local library.) Begin by teaching the sign-language alphabet. After you've taught the letters, sign the children's names and ask youngsters to identify whose name you are spelling each time. In addition to the alphabet, youngsters will enjoy learning and using the signs for simple words such as yes, no, or drink.

Dawn Moore–Preschool, Mount View Elementary, Thorndike, ME

"I'm The Baker!"

Bake up a batch of visual-discrimination skills with this fun group activity. To prepare, trace a class supply of cookie-cutter shapes onto poster board. Cut out the shapes. Decorate one side of each poster-board cookie. During circle time, have each child select a cookie cutter from among those you used to trace the cutouts. Hold up the undecorated sides of the cutouts one at a time, each time asking, "Whose cookie cutter made this cookie?" Invite the child who holds the corresponding cookie cutter to respond, "I'm the baker!" Ask him to then identify the object represented by the outline shape. Turn the cutout around to reveal the poster-board cookie's decorated side. Give the cutout to the child to hold until the end of the game. For a tasty variation, try playing this game with real cookies!

Karen Eiben—Preschool, The Kids' Place, LaSalle, IL

"That's My Name!"

What's in a name? Some circle-time fun! Print each child's name on a colored sentence strip or a strip of bulletin-board paper. Laminate the strips for durability. Begin each morning's routine by holding up the children's name strips one at a time. Encourage each child to greet you when he sees his name card. Then return his greeting. Vary this morning ritual by requesting a seasonal hello, such as "Gobble, gobble!" or "Ho, ho, ho!" Or ask the children to answer a question of the day—such as "What is your favorite color?"—when they see their names. Little ones will pay attention to roll call and quickly learn to recognize their own and their classmates' names.

Cheryl Kizer Ireland—Four- And Five-Year-Olds, St. Edward–Epiphany, Bon Air, VA

Share Bear

A special teddy bear will add a sense of closure to your end-of-the-day circle time. Designate a favorite stuffed teddy as "Share Bear." When you gather students at the end of the day, give each child an opportunity to hold Share Bear and describe a favorite activity of that day. Each youngster will leave your care with a happy memory to then share with Mom or Dad!

Elaine M. Utt—Two-Year-Olds, La Petite Academy, Tampa, FL

Birthday Whoop-De-Do!

Have a birthday to celebrate? Then start the day out on a happy note with this birthday song. In advance personalize a party horn for each child. During a group time, give each child a horn; then invite the birthday child to stand in front of the class. Lead your little ones in singing the following song; then have them blow their horns at the end of the song. Collect the horns; then store them in a gift-wrapped box for use during future birthday celebrations.

Today's A Special Day
*(sung to the tune of
"Head, Shoulders, Knees, And Toes")*

Today's a special day for you.
Just for you!
Today's a special day for you.
Just for you!
You're one year older.
Whoop-de, whoop-de-do!
Happy birthday!
Hooray for you!
Whoop-de-do!   *(Blow horn.)*

Lisa Leonardi
Norfolk, MA

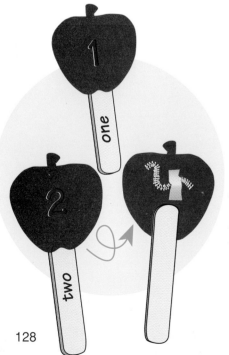

Ten Red Apples

Seeing a worm on one of these apples won't spoil the fun of this fingerplay and numeral-recognition activity. To prepare, tape one apple-shaped cutout to each of ten craft sticks. Write a different numeral from 1 to 10 on each of the apples. Then write the corresponding number word on each craft stick. Bend a green pipe cleaner to resemble a worm. Tape the worm to the back of an apple so that it is hidden. During a group time, ask ten volunteers to each hold an apple. Have the remaining children join you in reciting the following fingerplay; then have them guess the apple that has the worm by naming its number.

Ten red apples growing on a tree.   *(Hold up ten fingers.)*
Five for you and five for me.   *(Show one hand; then the other.)*
There's one little worm that you can't see. *(Wiggle one finger.)*
Where, oh where, could that little worm be? *(Hold hands out questioning.)*

Karen Eiben—Three- And Four-Year-Olds
The Kids' Place Child Development Center, LaSalle, IL

Holiday Countdown

Heighten anticipation of upcoming holidays with holiday countdown chains. Make a paper chain (one link for each day until the featured holiday) from construction paper. Attach the chain to a seasonal cutout and display it in the classroom. Each day during circle time, have a different child cut a link from the chain. When the last link is cut, it's holiday time!

Doris Weeaks—Four-Year-Olds
Walnut Ridge Baptist Church
Mansfield, TX

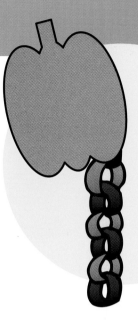

Jack-O-Shapes

Carve up some jack-o'-lantern fun with this circle-time game. Prior to a group time, hide jack-o'-lantern cutouts around the classroom; then lead youngsters in singing the following song as they set out to find the cutouts. When each child locates a cutout, have him return with it to the circle area. Then invite each youngster to describe where he found his smiling pumpkin cutout.

(sung to the tune of "Itsy-Bitsy Spider")
Funny jack-o'-lantern,
Where are you hiding?
Are you over here?
Or are you under there?
I will keep on looking, until I find you.
Funny jack-o'-lantern,
There you are!

D. Lyn Stevens—Preschool, A. M. Chaffee, Oxford, MA

Who's That Ghost?

Your little spooks will love this ghostly guessing game. Seat youngsters in a circle. Choose a volunteer to stand away from the circle and close his eyes. Invite another volunteer to be the ghost. Place a sheet with eye openings over the ghost's head; then have him stand in the center of the circle. Instruct the first child to return to the circle and try to guess "whoooooooooo's" under the sheet!

129

A Pleasant, Present Surprise

Surprise your little ones with this holiday guessing game. To prepare, turn a large box upside down; then wrap the sides and top with holiday paper. Top the box with a large bow. During a group time, ask a volunteer to close his eyes. Then ask a second volunteer to hide under the gift-wrapped box. Ask the first child to open his eyes, then look at the remaining children in the group. Provide him with plenty of chances to guess the child who is under the box, giving him clues if necessary. When the identity of the child under the box is guessed, have that child return to the group and close his eyes. Continue play as a new volunteer hides under the box. Aren't holiday surprises fun?

Pat Smith—Four-Year-Olds
Bells Elementary
Bells, TX

Creative Communication

Believe it or not, pudding can help your youngsters learn to communicate! To prepare for this delicious group activity, pour one or two boxes of pudding and the required amount of milk into a clean coffee can. Secure the lid on the can with a strip of duct tape. Seat the class in a circle on the floor. Pose a question, such as "What is your name?", or ask a theme-related question, such as "What do you like to do in the snow?" Roll the can to a child; then ask that child to answer the question. Next direct the child to roll the can to another member of the group. Continue until each child has answered the question. Then open the can and serve the pudding in small paper cups. Next question, please!

Mary Lauffenburger—Preschool
Warren Forest Company Head Start
Warren, PA

Wee Wisdom

This class book is sure to provide parents with many smiles and laughs of delight. Bind a supply of blank pages between construction-paper covers. Title the book "The World According To Us"; then decorate the cover. On the first page of the book, list the names of your young philosophers. Then, during group times, pose a question to your class. Write the question on a page in the book; then record each child's response. When the book is complete, send it home with a different child each night. It won't be long before parents request volume two of this charming book.

Christine Hartlieb—Four-Year-Olds
Junior Junction Childcare Center at St. Elizabeth's Hospital
Utica, NY

It's Better To Give

Youngsters will experience the joy of giving with this simple activity. To prepare, cut out a supply of pictures from a toy catalog. Glue each picture onto a square of wrapping paper. Place the pictures in a gift-wrapped box. During a group time, ask a child to select a gift from the box, decide the member of the class who would enjoy that gift, and then give that child the present. Continue until each child has given and received a gift.

Faith M. Tidd—Pre-K
Cohocton Head Start
Cohocton, NY

Christmas Cheer

Parents will enjoy this unique gift idea that records your class's Christmas cheer! Begin by audiotaping a holiday greeting to parents; then name each child in the class. During group times record your class singing their favorite holiday songs. When the tape is complete, duplicate a copy for each parent. Gift wrap the tapes; then send one home with each child. It's beginning to *sound* a lot like Christmas!

Kim Richman—Preschool
The Learning Zone
Des Moines, IA

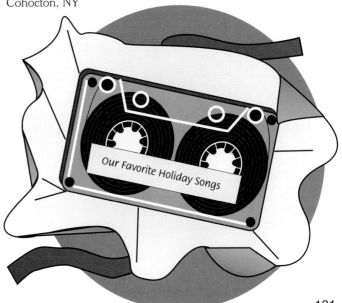

IT'S CIRCLE TIME!

Wiggle Your Fingers, Stomp Your Feet

Use this movement poem to invite youngsters to wiggle and stomp right into your morning circle time.

Wiggle your fingers in the air.
Wiggle them, wiggle them everywhere!

Stomp your feet upon the ground.
Stomp them, stomp them all around!

Now sit down and cross your feet.
Hands in laps all nice and neat.

Now we're ready to start our day.
We'll listen first, and then we'll play!

Sandy Curtis—Pre-K
Browncraft Day Care Center
Rochester, NY

Chinese New Year Parade

Turn your group time into a celebration by planning a parade. To follow this Chinese New Year's custom, you'll need a dragon, of course. To make one, use fabric paints to paint colorful designs or Chinese symbols on a white sheet. Cover a shoebox, the shoebox lid, and a medium-sized box with bulletin-board paper. Turn the larger box upside down; then cut eyeholes in it. Hot-glue the shoebox and lid below the eyeholes for a mouth. Use markers, crepe-paper streamers, and paper to decorate the boxes to resemble a dragon. Lastly, hot-glue the sheet to the box.

Invite several children to stand under the dragon; then provide the remaining children with rhythm sticks. Lead the group in a parade as you shout Happy New Year in Chinese: *"Gung-Hey-Fat-Choy!"*

Sam Ferguson—Four- And Five-Year-Olds
St. Joseph Child Development Center
Louisville, KY

Flannelboard Gingerbread Men

Catch these gingerbread men for your flannelboard and you'll have a fun way to reinforce shapes and colors. To prepare, cut four large gingerbread-man shapes from brown felt. Use wiggle eyes and a marker or felt to add facial features to the cutouts; then glue a different color of ricrac around the edge of each one. For each gingerbread cutout, cut three felt buttons that are the same color as the cutout's ricrac, making sure that each set of buttons is a different geometric shape. Following a telling of the Gingerbread Man story, invite youngsters to match the buttons to the flannelboard gingerbread men. Your group will catch on to counting, colors, and shapes as fast as they can!

Lucille Ann Ingrassia—Two-Year-Olds Integrated,
 Special Education/Day Care
Just Kids Learning Center
Middle Island, NY

Musical Patterns

Need a quick circle-time activity? Pull out your supply of rhythm instruments. Ask two volunteers at a time to each choose an instrument. Have the two children stand in front of the group. Then suggest a musical pattern for them to play. Tap, ding! Tap, ding! Tap, ding! Now that's a pattern that's music to your ears!

The Baker Says

This adaptation of Simon Says bakes up a batch of youngsters who are great at following directions. To play, you'll need a tagboard cookie cutout for each child and one baker's hat. (Use a real hat, or make one by stapling white tissue paper to a sentence-strip headband.) Don the hat; then give each child a cookie cutout. Remind students that all directions preceded by the phrase "The baker says" should be followed. Then begin the game by giving directions involving the cutouts. For example, you might say, "The baker says put your cookie on the ground," or "The baker says tap your cookie with your left foot." Invite group members to don the hat and take turns being the baker. Just for fun, give youngsters real cookies. The baker says *eat* your cookies!

Henry Fergus—Preschool
Buckeye Elementary School District #33
Buckeye, AZ

133

Cupid, Cupid

Here's a lovely valentine's game for your preschoolers! Choose a student to be Cupid and give him a Cupid's headband. Ask Cupid to hide his eyes while you give another child a valentine card to hide in her lap. When the card is out of sight, have Cupid uncover his eyes while his classmates say, "Cupid, Cupid, where's your valentine?" Help Cupid guess who has his valentine. Then have the child hiding the valentine become the next Cupid.

Cracker-Crumb Dance

This action song is sure to get enthusiastic reviews from your little snackers! After a cracker snack for everyone, get rid of those pesky crumbs by singin' and movin' to the beat. Crunch and munch—we love crackers, crumbs and all!

(sung to the tune of "Frère Jacques")

Graham crackers,
Animal crackers,
Soda crackers too.
Soda crackers too.
They make such a crumbly mess. *(Brush hands together.)*
They make such a crumbly mess.
What to do? *(Turn palms up.)*
What to do?

Brush your shirt off, *(Brush imaginary crumbs off clothing.)*
Dust your pants off,
Stomp your feet! *(Stomp feet.)*
Stomp your feet!
Do the cracker-crumb dance. *(Dance in place.)*
Do the cracker-crumb dance.
Shimmy and shake! *(Shimmy and shake.)*
Shimmy and shake!

adapted from an idea by Diane Z. Shore
Marietta, GA

Bear, Bear, Spring Is Here!

If you're ready for spring, play this group game with all of your little cubs! Use blankets over a couple of chairs to create a bear cave. Have the children sit in a circle near the cave's opening. Ask one child to be a bear, sleeping in the cave. As soon as the bear is slumbering, give another child a bunch of berries (pom-poms or beads) to hide in her lap. When the berries are hidden, have the children call out, "Bear, bear, spring is here!" Encourage the bear to wake up and come out of the cave, then guess who is hiding the berries. Have the child caught with the berries become the bear and continue play. Who's ready for spring?

Diane DiMarco—Preschool
Country Kids Preschool And Child Care Center
Groton, MA

Cattle Roundup

During Western Days or a farm unit, corral a small group of your aspiring cowhands for this cow-counting card game. To prepare, die-cut up to 80 cow cutouts. Glue one, two, or three cutouts on each of 15 cards. In the center of a circle of three or four children, place the cards facedown—along with the remaining cow cutouts. Give each player a piece of twine or yarn to loop into a corral for his cattle. To play, have each cowpoke in turn take a card, then put a matching number of cow cutouts in his corral. Continue play for four or more rounds. At the end of the game, have each cowpoke count the number of cows in his corral. Get along, little dogies!

adapted from an idea by Charlet Keller—Pre-K
ICC Elementary Preschool, Violet Hill, AR

Alphabet Walk

Put a little rhythm into letter recognition with this musical game. In advance, fill a bag with initial-sound cards. Place alphabet letters in a circle on the floor. Instruct the children to walk or dance around the circle when the music plays and stop immediately beside a letter when the music stops. Start some lively music, stopping it when the children least expect it. Draw a card from the bag, show it to the children, and say the picture word and the name of its initial letter. Ask the children to identify the child standing by the matching letter in the circle. When the music stops next time and it's time to pull another card from the bag, invite that child to do the honors. Here we go again. Listen carefully!

Beth Walker—Four- And Five-Year-Olds
BCC Child Development Center, Melbourne, FL

IT'S CIRCLE TIME!

The Sharing Song

Sharing comes straight from the heart as youngsters play this circle-time game. Seat children in a circle. Give a construction-paper heart cutout to each of three students. Have these three children walk around the outside of the circle while everyone sings the following song. At the end of the song, have each child give his heart to someone seated in the circle and exchange places with that child. Repeat the activity until everyone has had a chance to share. How sweet!

(sung to the tune of "London Bridge")

I am learning how to share, how to share, how to share.
I am learning how to share. This heart's for you.

Debbie Brown—Four- And Five-Year-Olds
Corson Park Daycare
Millville, NJ

Circle-Time Drive-In

Invite children to drive up to circle time and learn the feature presentation of personal space with this idea. Collect a class supply of duplicating-paper boxes. Cut the bottom out of each box. Have each child use paint, construction paper, scissors, and glue to make her box into a vehicle. Prior to circle time, give children a chance to "drive" around the room; then ask them to park at the circle. Have students remain in their vehicles during circle time to reinforce the idea of personal space. Soon the vehicles won't be necessary at circle time and can be used for outside play. Vroom, vroom!

Lynn Colbert—Preschool
Astor Center For Child Development
Bronx, NY

Circle Seating

Here's a fun way to assess your little ones' color- and shape-recognition abilities and create a favorable seating arrangement at the same time. In advance, cut geometric shapes from colored construction paper; then laminate them for durability. When it's circle time, arrange the shape cutouts in a circle on the floor. Invite each child to your group area by asking her to find and sit on a specific shape. For example, say, "Courtney, find an orange circle." For a challenging variation, add numerals or letters to the shapes. A transition time full of learning!

Christa Wimberly—Four-Year-Olds
All Saints Preschool
Albuquerque, NM

Pat-a-cake, pat-a-cake, baker's man,
Bake me a cake as fast as you can.
Roll it and shape it and mark it with a [G],
And put it in the oven for [Grover] and me!

Bake Me A Name

First names are delicious in this circle-time game. Gather wooden, plastic, magnetic, or cookie-cutter letters. Put the letters in a bag or bowl. Review the traditional rhyme "Pat-A-Cake" with your little ones. Then have one child draw a letter from the bag or bowl. Ask whose name begins with the selected letter. Lead the group in reciting the rhyme again—this time replacing the "*B*" and "Baby" with the chosen letter and a child's name that begins with that letter. Continue until all of your children's names have been inserted into the rhyme.

Terry Steinke—Preschool
Emmaus Lutheran School
Indianapolis, IN

"Egg-ceptional" Singing

Need a time filler? Just crack open one of these eggs! To prepare, ask your little ones to name their favorite circle-time songs and fingerplays. Write each title on a small piece of paper; then tuck each piece into a plastic egg. Keep the eggs in an Easter basket in your group area. When you need a quick time filler, just ask a child to crack open an egg. Read the title aloud; then sing the song. To ease transitions, this "eggs-cellent" idea just can't be beat!

Jane FitzSimmons-Thomez—Preschool
St. Mary's Preschool
Owatonna, MN

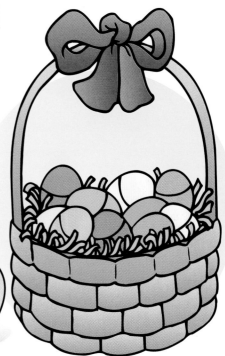

The Bunny Hop Song

Jumping Waves

Refine your youngsters' muscle control and create a wave of giggles with this lively game. Hold one end of a jump rope and have another adult hold the opposite end so that the rope is stretched out between you and is close to the ground. Make waves by gently shaking the rope up and down. Next challenge each child, in turn, to jump over the waves, being careful not to "wipe out" by touching the rope. After each child has had a turn, raise the rope slightly higher than before. This game is sure to have your little ones jumping with joy!

Lori Kent
Hood River, OR

Skill-Building Aquariums

There's nothing fishy about this activity that has youngsters following directions while sharpening their color-recognition and counting skills. Give each child in a small group a sterilized, blue Styrofoam® tray (aquarium) and ten colorful paper fish. Next give the group various directions to follow, such as "Place three fish in your aquarium" or "If you have a yellow fish or a blue fish, put it in your aquarium." Encourage your little ones to take their fish and aquariums home, then share this activity with their families.

Susan Luengen—Preschool Special Education
Makalapa School
Honolulu, HI

Transition Chant

For a smooth transition into circle time, have your little ones perform this charming chant.

Sit like a butterfly.   (Sit with legs crossed.)
Buzz like a bee.   (Make buzzing noises.)
Shake your head like a monkey in a tree.   (Shake head.)
Put your hands down on your knees.   (Put hands on knees.)
Make your mouth like a fish in the sea.   (Pucker lips.)

Wanda Odom—Pre-K
Waller Elementary
Youngstown, FL

Setting The Stage:
Interest Areas And Centers

Setting The Stage:

Block Center

A House For Me

These charming additions to your block area will help youngsters learn their addresses as well as develop the concept of community. Purchase a class supply plus some extra of freestanding wooden house shapes (available at craft stores). Invite each child to paint a house; then allow the paint to dry. Use a permanent marker to write each child's name and address on her house; then coat each house with nontoxic varnish. When the varnish is dry, add the houses and a supply of toy vehicles to your block area. Encourage youngsters to build neighborhoods; then, as the children play, point out the names and addresses on the houses. Later add additional houses painted to resemble other familiar places, such as your preschool, stores, and fast-food restaurants. What a busy neighborhood!

Liz Novak—Preschool, Pumpkin Patch Preschool And Playcare, Davenport, IA

Sensory Table

Road Construction

Your sensory area will be humming with the sounds of bulldozers and backhoes when you add some road-construction props. Fill your sensory table with soil. Add some small rocks and sticks, along with a supply of toy construction vehicles. Spray the soil with water to keep it moist and pliable; then watch your crew of workers dig in.

Claudia V. Tábora—Preschool
Como Community Child Care, Minneapolis, MN

Literacy Center

Alpha-Boards

These personalized workmats and plaster letters spell out fun at your literacy center. Cut the fronts and backs from cereal boxes so that you have a class supply of cardboard mats. Personalize the blank side of a mat for each child. Laminate the mats. Using Faster Plaster™ and alphabet-shaped candy molds, make enough letters so that each child has the letters needed to spell his name. Store each child's set of letters in a separate, labeled berry basket. Put the workmats and baskets in a center. At the center, a child chooses a workmat and the corresponding set of letters. He then matches the letters to the letters on the mat to spell his name or a classmate's name.

Bonnie McKenzie—Pre-K And Gr. K
Cheshire Country Day School, Cheshire, CT

Interest Areas And Centers

Water Table

Getting The Worm

Youngsters are sure to wiggle right over to your water center when they discover that it has been inhabited by worms—rubber worms that is! Purchase a number of rubber worms from the fishing department of a discount store. Put the worms in your table; then fill it with water and a squirt or two of washable brown paint so that the water looks muddy. Add buckets, small fishnets, and paper towels to the center. Invite youngsters to reach in and have a slimy good time!

Cindy Lawson—Toddlers And Preschool
Shell Lake, WI

Manipulatives Center

Tabletop Flannelboard

Transform an unused table into an instant flannelboard with this handy idea. Cut a piece of felt to match the dimensions of a small tabletop. Use double-sided tape to attach the piece to the tabletop. Place the flannelboard table in a center along with a variety of felt shapes, numerals, and letters.

Nancy Wolfgram—Two-Year-Olds
KinderCare Learning Center #1111
Lincoln, NE

Games Center

Farm Animal Slapjack

Bring the farmyard to your games center with this variation of the card game Slapjack. To prepare a game for two players, attach a different farm-animal sticker on each of eight index cards. Laminate the cards if desired.

To play, a pair of children sit facing each other with the cards faceup between them. The teacher names a color, characteristic, or type of animal, or makes the sound of an animal. Each partner then tries to be the first to slap the appropriate card. The first child to slap the correct animal card keeps the card. Continue the game until all the cards have been slapped. The partners then count their cards to determine a winner.

Jeri Ashford, Granite School District, Salt Lake City, UT

Setting The Stage:

Water Table

Bobbing Jack-O'-Lanterns

Your youngsters will have a ball when strengthening fine-motor skills at this seasonal center. Use a black permanent marker to draw jack-o'-lantern faces on a quantity of orange Ping-Pong® balls; then float the balls in your water table. Place a fishnet (or large spoon) and a jack-o'-lantern bucket nearby. Using one hand, a child manipulates the net to scoop the jack-o'-lanterns, then drops them into the bucket. For a variation, encourage a youngster to use his other hand or to wear a blindfold.

Beth Jones—Junior Kindergarten
Stevensville School
Stevensville, Ontario, Canada

Block Area

Block Buildup

Math skills will really stack up with this constructive idea. Trace blocks of a variety of shapes and sizes onto pieces of construction paper; then program each shape with a different numeral. Cut out the shapes; then laminate them for durability. Tape the cutouts to the floor of your block area. Challenge youngsters to build block towers that correspond to each cutout's shape and numeral. This center is a blockbuster!

Maggie Woldum—Preschool
Head Start Preschool
Bozeman, MT

Manipulatives Center

Bushel Of Leaf Fun

Youngsters will rake up lots of sorting and classification practice with this interactive display. Collect leaves from several different types of trees. Laminate each leaf. Mount a fall character on a background. Gather as many miniature plastic baskets as you have types of leaves, plus one extra. Attach one different type of leaf to the front of each basket. Staple the baskets to the board. Store the laminated leaves in the extra basket. To use, a student sorts the leaves into the correct baskets. What a bushel of fun!

Wilma Droegemueller—Preschool
Zion Lutheran School
Mt. Pulaski, IL

Interest Areas And Centers

Games Center

Profile Puzzles

Shape up visual-discrimination skills with these fun puzzles. Gather collections of small items. Arrange each collection on a piece of poster board; then use a black marker to trace around each item's shape. Laminate if desired. To use a puzzle, a child places each object from a collection on its corresponding outline.

Sharon Washer—Four- And Five-Year-Olds
Bolivar-Richburg Preschool
Bolivar, NY

Sensory Table

Seasonal Sensation

What's orange and black and creeping with spiders? The contents of your sensory table when you fill it with orange and black shredded paper (available at party-supply stores) and a quantity of plastic spiders. Encourage a child to find the spiders, then count them. Your little ones are sure to love this sensory-table surprise!

Susan Burbridge—Four-Year-Olds
Colonial Hills United Methodist School
San Antonio, TX

Science Center

Pick-A-Pocket

This idea will spark curiosity and keep your science center neatly organized at the same time. Hang a shoe organizer with clear pockets near your science table. Fill the pockets with materials to investigate such as feathers, seashells, pinecones, rocks, twigs, and leaves. Also place magnifying glasses in several pockets. Now observation and exploration materials are clearly visible, and cleanup is a breeze!

Jodi Sykes—Pre-K
North Grade
Lake Worth, FL

Setting The Stage:

Housekeeping Area

Deck The Halls!

This holiday season provide youngsters with everything they will need to festively decorate your housekeeping area. In a large box, place realistic pine garland, wreaths, bows, stockings, battery-operated candles, and other extra decorating items you might have. Consider setting up a small, artificial tree along with a supply of easy-to-hang, unbreakable ornaments. Encourage youngsters to use the items to decorate the area. When cleanup time arrives, assist them in carefully returning all the decorations to the box.

Games Area

Magnet Mania

Little ones are sure to be attracted to your classroom games area when you stock it with these inexpensive magnet boards. Obtain several countertop protectors from the housewares department of your favorite store. Along with the boards, place a supply of letter- and numeral-shaped magnets in the center. Or attach magnetic tape to the backs of laminated game pieces to use with the boards. Students will get stuck on the fun!

Teresa Hanak—Three-Year-Olds, Fenton Preschool
Fenton, MI

Woodworking Center

Hammers And Nails

Stumped for a way to add variety to your woodworking center? Add an old stump or a large log! Students who visit the center can hammer nails into the stump. If your center is stocked with small pieces of wood, students can also nail these to the stump. And of course, remember to provide safety goggles, establish guidelines, and monitor the center closely when it is in use.

Tanya Rowburrey—Preschool, Milton, FL

Interest Areas And Centers

Water Table

Gone Four-Wheelin'

To create perfect conditions for winter driving, squirt mounds of shaving cream into an empty water table. Your little ones will love plowing through the snow with toy vehicles to get to their imagined destinations. There's "snow" telling what will occur in this blizzard of activity.

Joan Banker—Three- And Four-Year-Olds
St. Mary's Child Development Center
Garner, NC

Manipulatives Center

Tabletop Menorah

Sharpen your children's patterning skills with this enlightening suggestion! Use masking tape or colored tape to make a menorah design on a tabletop. Have your children create their own unique patterns along the design using a variety of math counters. As you admire a student's work, ask her to describe the attribute she used for patterning. Your little ones will light up when it's their turn at this festive center!

Nancy Barad—Four-Year-Olds
Bet Yeladim Preschool And Kindergarten
Columbia, MD

Reading Area

A Good Book And A Warm Fire

There's nothing better than curling up with a good book on a cold winter's day. To create this mood in your reading area, cut corrugated board that has a brick design (found at craft stores) to resemble a fireplace. Mount it on a wall. Stack cardboard blocks that look like bricks at the bottom of the fireplace to make a hearth. Add stockings, a rug, a teddy bear, and a rocking chair to your scene along with seasonal reading selections. Little ones will want to warm up to reading! This scenery also makes a terrific backdrop for holiday pictures to give as gifts to parents.

Joan Banker—Three- And Four-Year-Olds

Season's Greetings

Setting The Stage:

Block Center

Tending The Garden

Cultivate the roots of your little ones' imaginations with this fun garden idea. Encourage students to make garden rows with blocks. Provide an assortment of plastic vegetables for the children to "plant" around, on top of, and under the blocks. Have children's garden tools and baskets nearby for the harvest. There is sure to be lots of class-grown fun in this bountiful block garden. Don't be surprised if a produce stand is the next thing in demand!

Linda Blassingame—Pre-K And Gr. K
JUST 4 & 5 Developmental Laboratory
Mobile, AL

Art Center

Suddenly Salad

Give youngsters an opportunity to create an enticing salad while developing fine-motor skills. Stock the center with scalloped sheets of green paper in various shades to represent lettuce. Add an assortment of construction-paper, vegetable-shaped cutouts; play dough; scissors; and plastic bowls.

To make a salad, a student tears the green paper into "bite-size" pieces and puts them in a bowl. She then uses scissors to cut up her choice of vegetable cutouts to add to her salad. If any other vegetables or toppings are desired, encourage her to mold these from play dough, then use them to garnish her salad.

If desired, invite the child to carry her salad over to the housekeeping center. Provide empty salad-dressing bottles, tongs, and plastic forks for a pretend feast. These salads are scrumptious skill builders, any way you toss them!

Linda Blassingame—Pre-K And Gr. K

Dramatic Play Area

Visiting The Vet

Celebrate National Pet Week (the first full week in May) by converting your dramatic play area into a veterinarian clinic. Bring in pet carriers or cut boxes to resemble animal cages. Put a toy doctor's kit in the area as well as other props—such as masks, rubber gloves, paper, pencils, and a clipboard. Also include a roll of gauze and an elastic bandage wrap for treating the "injured." Invite youngsters to bring stuffed animals from home to fill the clinic with patients. (Be sure to tag each toy pet with its owner's name.) Is there a doctor in the house?

Colleen Keller—Preschool And Prep-K
Clarion-Goldfield Elementary, Clarion, IA

Math Area

Counting Strips

String up some counting fun with these counting strips! To make one, cut sturdy cardboard into a 3" x 8" strip. Write a numeral on the left side of the strip. To the right of the numeral, punch a hole; then draw a row of the corresponding number of dots. Cut a one-inch slit in the center of the right edge of the strip. Cut a 12-inch length of heavy string; then wrap a small piece of tape around one end and knot the other end. Thread the knotted end of the string through the hole; then tape it to the back of the strip. Finally cut out a variety of geometric shapes from meat trays. Punch a hole in the middle of each shape.

For independent counting practice, a child chooses a strip, reads the numeral on the strip, and threads the same amount of shapes onto the string. To secure the shapes, he pulls the end of the string through the slit. One, two, three, a good counter he will be!

Carol Pochert—Four- And Five-Year-Olds, ABC Kids Care, Grafton, WI

Discovery Area

Start Your Engines

Your children will zoom over to this magnetic raceway to practice hand/eye coordination. Draw and color a racetrack on a large piece of tagboard. Then draw, color, and cut out several car outlines from tagboard. Laminate the track and the cars. Slide a large paper clip onto each car. Tape the ends of the tagboard raceway to the edges of two tables so that the track is suspended in air. Place the cars on the track. Invite a child to use the raceway by moving a magnet underneath the tagboard. On your mark, get set, go!

Kim Richman—Preschool
The Learning Zone, Des Moines, IA

Water Table

Rain, Rain, Go Away

If you teach in a church-affiliated day care or preschool, use April's rainy weather as an inspiration to recall the story of Noah. Then add a toy ark (or boat) and lots of toy animals to the water table so children can reenact the miraculous event. For added effect, provide little ones with a prism to use with the water and sunlight to create a rainbow for the promise of a better day.

Setting The Stage:

Science Center

Rain Forest

Little ones will think they are actually in the Amazon when you transform an area of your room into a tropical rain forest. To create a rain-forest canopy, drape a large piece of camouflage net (the kind used for hunting) over any furniture in the area. Randomly place plastic or rubber snakes, frogs, crocodiles, and lizards in the netting and around the center. Also place artificial trees, vines, and plants in the center. Play a recording of rain-forest sounds (available from nature stores). Let the adventure begin!

Glenda C. Roddey
An Academe For Children, Inc.
Springdale, AR

Block Center

Creative Block Fun

Give your block center a new twist with this fun idea. Purchase several yards of different-colored, sheer gauzy fabric. Cut the fabric into a variety of sizes. Encourage youngsters who build houses in the center to drape the fabric pieces over the blocks to make doors or windows. Let their imaginations be their guide!

Amy Laubis
Children's Garden Preschool
Kenton, OH

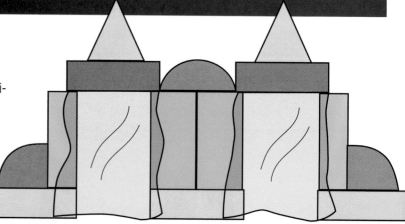

Dramatic Play Area

Preschool Hair-Cuttery

Your students won't recognize the dramatic play area when you convert it into a hair salon. Glue photos of children (preferably your students) with different hair styles to sheets of construction paper. Also mount pictures of blow-dryers, scissors, and hair supplies on separate sheets of construction paper; then laminate the pages. Place the pages between two tagboard covers and bind the pages to make a book. Write the name of the hair salon on the cover of the book. Place the book, chairs, mirrors, empty shampoo bottles, towels, rollers, barrettes, ribbons, combs or brushes, and empty hairspray bottles in the center. Also stock the center with Styrofoam® heads (used by beauticians) and several wigs. To the front of the center, tape a sign that reads "The Preschool Hair-Cuttery." To use the center, have little ones pretend to be barbers or beauticians. Wash and set?

Karen Eiben—Three-Year-Olds
The Kid's Place
La Salle, IL

Interest Areas And Centers

Sand Table

Baskets Full Of Fun!

Enrich your sand table with this hands-on idea. Half-fill your table with colored plastic grass. Place several baskets, small plastic chicks and bunnies, and plastic eggs in the grass. To use this center, have little ones use the materials provided to create nifty spring baskets!

Mary Borreca—Preschool
Martinsville, TX

Water Table

Laundry Table

Set your water table outside and convert it into a laundry table. Half-fill the table with warm water; then add a scoop of mild laundry soap. In a laundry basket near the table, provide clothespins and small cloth items such as old handkerchiefs, doll clothing, and socks. Mount a clothesline between two chairs near the table, or set up a clothes-drying rack. To use this center, a child takes a piece of clothing from the laundry basket and washes it in the laundry table. (If desired, add an additional tub of water for rinsing.) He then wrings the excess water from the piece of clothing and uses a clothespin to clip it to the clothesline. Rub-a-dub-dub!

Reading Center

A Reading Pond

Create a setting in your reading area that your youngsters will dive into—a reading pond! To make a reading pond, place a round blue tablecloth on the floor of a wading pool to resemble water. Randomly place round green pillows in the pond to represent lily pads. Also place turtle and fish puppets in and around the pond. Position live or artificial plants around the pond area. On a table near the pond, provide books about pond life, plus frog headbands or hats. To use this center, allow two children at a time to don frog hats, choose books from the table, and enjoy reading in the reading pond. No doubt this center will make a splash!

Kate Taluga—Preschool
Big Bend Community Coordinated Child Care
Tallahassee, FL

Life In A Small Pond

Setting The Stage:

Dramatic Play Area

Behind The "Sea-nes"

Under the sea? Well, not quite. With this dramatic play prop, you'll have to change the words of that popular song to *behind* the sea. To make this exciting sea scene, use clear Con-Tact® covering to secure pictures of ocean life to a clear shower curtain. Then hang the curtain from the ceiling near a dramatic play area or a science center that has a sea-life focus. Add materials such as snorkeling gear and books about ocean life to the area. Get ready for some dramatic ocean-life exploration!

Karen Beary—Preschool
The Children's Center
Kingston, MA

Games Center

"Cowabunga" Cow Bowling

Your little ones will be "udderly" delighted to make and play this bowling game. Collect a supply of empty, clean milk or juice cartons. Seal the lids. Mix a small amount of dishwashing liquid into an amount of white paint. Invite youngsters to paint the cartons white. Then, when the paint is dry, have students paint black spots on the cartons. To bowl, a student arranges the desired number of cartons randomly or in a triangle. (If desired suggest a number of cartons based on the child's abilities.) He then rolls a soft ball toward the cartons in order to knock them down. When he has knocked down all of the cartons, he or his bowling pals "moo." This game will keep 'em "moo-ving"!

Darlene V. Martino—Pre-K, Palmyra Head Start, Palmyra, NY

Sensory Table

Beads And Bowls

For a change of pace, fill a sensory table with lots of large beads and a supply of plastic containers and their lids. After students have enjoyed free exploration at the table, challenge them to fill the containers with specific colors or numbers of beads. Consider returning water or sand to the table *before* putting away the beads and containers. Stand back and watch as your little ones have fun and make discoveries, too!

Linda Kutach—Pre-K
Hutto Elementary
Hutto, TX

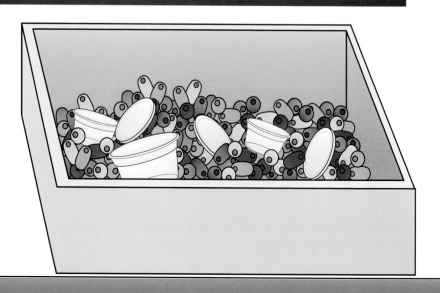

Interest Areas And Centers

Sand Table

Like Sand In An Hourglass…

Reuse an empty two-liter plastic soda bottle by turning it into a discovery toy for your sand or rice center. To make one, cut off the top third of a bottle. Invert the top portion of the bottle; then insert it into the bottom portion as shown. Tape the portions together, being sure to cover any rough edges. Encourage students to pour sand or rice into the funnel and watch as it fills the container. If desired cut windows on the side of the bottle for better peeking and faster emptying.

Heather Snider
Oklahoma City, OK

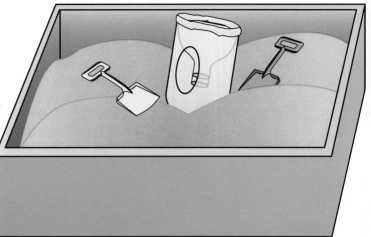

Math Center

All Sorts Of Fun

Use colored tape to divide a round or square table into a sorting area with two, three, or four sections. To encourage students to sort by color, tape a different-colored shape in each section if desired. Keep a variety of manipulatives nearby so that individual students or groups of students can come to the table for plenty of sorting fun.

Kim Hilario—Pre-Kindergarten
Adobe Christian Preschool
Petaluma, CA

Literacy Center

Meet The Press

Our sources tell us that this idea for developing literacy and language will make big news in your classroom. Transform your literacy center into a newsroom and television news set by stocking it with clipboards, blank paper, writing utensils, toy microphones, and old newspapers. To facilitate up-to-the-minute weather reports, add a map to the area. To encourage aspiring reporters and photographers, add toy cameras and broken real cameras to the center.

For extra fun make this paper camera that produces "instant" photos. Fold an 8" x 7" black paper rectangle in half; then glue the sides together. Add paper shapes as shown so that the pocket resembles a camera. Glue newspaper pictures to 3" x 5" index cards; then insert the cards into the pocket. To use the camera, a child pretends to take a picture. He then pulls out a card and describes the newsworthy scene.

Mary Lynn Storrie—Four-Year-Olds, St. James School, Louisville, KY

Water Table

Alphabet Quackers

Make a big splash with your little ones with this simple, yet fun, addition to your water table. Program the bottoms of a number of rubber-duck bath toys with numerals or letters. Float the ducks in your water table; then invite your little ones to take turns selecting a duck from the table and identifying the symbol written on it. As a challenge, have youngsters sequence the ducks by numeral or find ducks programmed with matching upper- and lowercase letters. Be sure to invite the children to enjoy some free water play, too!

Lonnie Murphy
Sarasota, FL

Manipulatives Area

Building Table

Put your LEGO® and DUPLO® blocks up on a pedestal with this unique idea. Glue LEGO® or DUPLO® building plates to the top of folding television tray tables. This sturdy, defined workspace makes it easy for little builders to create masterpieces. Storage is a snap—simply put the blocks in a container, and then fold up the table!

Amy Flori—Two- And Three-Year-Olds
Christ Methodist Child Development Center
Venice, FL

Dramatic-Play Area

Preschool Posy Shop

Your children's color-recognition, sorting, and counting skills are sure to bloom when you transform your dramatic-play area into a posy shop! Ask parents to donate old artificial flowers, vases, and flowerpots; then place the items in your center along with seed packets, paper, markers, and play money. Encourage children playing in the center to count the flowers and sort them by color. Also encourage literacy by having workers make price tags and signs for the store. Now that's some bloomin' good fun!

Colleen Keller—Preschool And Pre-K
Clarion-Goldfield Elementary
Clarion, IA

Getting Your Ducklings In A Row

Tips For Getting Organized

Getting Your Ducklings

Mega-Sized Mouse Pads

Give your preschoolers the advantage of an extra-large mouse pad while they're learning to use computers and honing their fine-motor skills. Replace your mouse pad with a sheet of craft foam, securing the foam to your table or cart with double-sided tape. Since children can move the mouse over a much wider area, they'll be able to focus more on the computer activity itself.

adapted from an idea by Patricia W. Mitchell, Eastbrook Elementary School, Winter Park, FL

Stylish Center Management

Manage your centers in style with this personalized T-shirt system. Cut a class supply of people shapes from tagboard; then write a different child's name on each one. For each center, also cut out the same number of people shapes as you will allow children in that center at one time. Next cut a class supply of T-shirt shapes from tagboard. Personalize each T-shirt; then have each child use crayons to color his T-shirt and his person shape. To make a starting chart, glue the decorated people shapes to a sheet of poster board. For each center sign, label a piece of poster board with a center's name; then glue the same number of people shapes to the sign as you will allow children in that center at one time. Laminate the starting chart, the center signs, and the T-shirts. Finally, attach the hook side of a piece of Velcro® to the back of each T-shirt, and the loop side of a piece of Velcro® to each person shape on the starting chart and the center signs. Attach the shirts to the chart; then display the chart in a group area. Display the center signs in the centers so they are within students' reach.

To use the system, a child takes his T-shirt off the starting chart, and then attaches it to a person shape on the sign in the center of his choice. When each person shape on a sign is wearing a shirt, that center is full.

Theresa Knapp—Preschool, Asbury Day Care Center, Rochester, NY

In A Row

Tips For Getting Organized

Window-Shade Wonder

With this clever idea, you'll have two display areas in the space of one, and a handy shelf, too! Construct a simple drapery cornice sized to fit over one of your existing bulletin boards. Paint the cornice as desired. When the paint is dry, bolt it to the wall over the bulletin board. Next use acrylic craft paints to create a display on a plain window shade. When the paint is dry, retract the shade; then mount it to the inside of the cornice (following package directions). To use the new display, pull the shade down; then retract it to use the bulletin board again.

Renee Farrand—Preschool
Union United Methodist Church Preschool/Kindergarten
Irmo, SC

Tissue-Box Storage Tip

Reuse empty tissue boxes as storage containers for learning-center pieces. You'll find their openings easily accommodate a child's small hands, yet prevent large spills. Gather a variety of empty tissue boxes. If desired, cover them with decorative Con-Tact® covering (being sure to keep the opening intact) or color-code them by centers. Drop game pieces, manipulatives, and other small center items into the boxes. At cleanup time, students simply return the items to the boxes, and the boxes to the centers.

Diane G. Williams
Seven Pines Elementary, Sandston, VA

Fish-Tank Viewing

Do you have an observation window so that adults can look into your classroom? If so, use this decorative idea to keep youngsters' attention focused inside the classroom rather than on the people outside the classroom. Tape blue cellophane to the outside of the window; then attach sea-life cutouts to the classroom side of the glass. Children who look at the window will tend to focus on the sea-life shapes, and observers' view of the room will remain clear.

Victoria Greco, Fairfield, OH

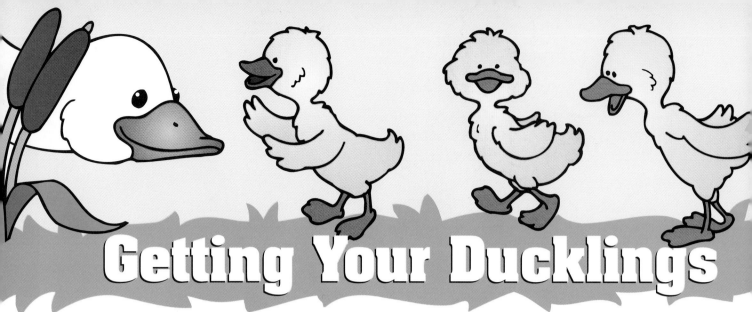

Getting Your Ducklings

Personal Portfolios

Enlist the help of children's families to decorate portfolio boxes for storage of students' work throughout the year. Collect a class supply of empty cereal boxes. Cut the top flaps off the boxes; then cover each box with paper. Personalize each box before sending it home along with a note suggesting that a parent help his child decorate the box. Hang the returned boxes on a clothesline in your room. When you want to save an item for a child's portfolio of work, simply slip the item into his box. What a decorative way to store your little ones' work!

Kim Spankowski—Four-Year-Olds
Kenosha Unified School District Head Start
Kenosha, WI

Chime Time

Smooth out transition-time turmoil with this musical idea. Ring a small wind chime to quietly signal transitions. The results will be music to your ears!

Michelle Espelien—Preschool
St. James Preschool
Burnsville, MN

Box It Up

Store small items—such as bulletin-board letters, stickers, and small manipulatives—in plastic videocassette boxes. Label each box with its contents; then store the boxes on a shelf or in a cupboard. A great idea— any way you stack it.

Amy Drake—Two-Year-Olds
Westview Childcare Ministry
Fort Wayne, IN

In A Row

Tips For Getting Organized

Sticky Solution

Do adhesives pull the paint off your classroom walls? If so, then try this idea. Adhere a piece of clear Con-Tact® covering to a wall where you'd like to display children's work. Then use tape or Sticky-Tac to secure children's work to the covering. What a neat solution to a sticky problem!

Michelle Miget—Four-Year-Olds
Humboldt Elementary
St. Joseph, MO

Banded Boxes

Keeping the lids on individual crayon boxes is a snap with this easy idea. Punch a hole in the center of a crayon box's lid. Slide a paper clip onto a rubber band. From the underside of the lid, thread the rubber band through the hole and pull it until the paper clip is flat against the lid. Secure the paper clip with a wide piece of tape. Place the lid on the box; then wrap the rubber band around the bottom of the box. Now crayons stay securely in their boxes and are easy to store.

Bernadette Hoyer—Pre-K
Howard B. Brunner School
Scotch Plains, NJ

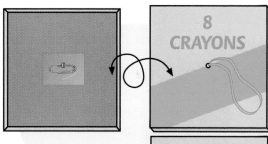

Seat Belt Matchup

Here's a tip that will help your little ones buckle up quickly and safely when riding in your center's van or bus. Affix matching stickers to the corresponding ends of each seat belt; then cover the stickers with clear tape. Each child can quickly identify his seat belt by simply matching the stickers. Getting safely seated is a snap!

Vail McCole—Pre-K
Tigger's Treehouse
Grand Junction, CO

Getting Your Ducklings

Puppets On A String

Need a clever way to store puppets? Here's a space-saving idea you can really hang on to! Hang a plastic chain with clips (available at discount stores) from your classroom ceiling. Clip the puppets available for student use on the part of the chain that is within youngsters' reach. Hang the remaining puppets higher on the chain.

Laura Sacco—Four-Year-Olds
East Woods School
Oyster Bay, NY

Sleepy-Time Wand

Help your little ones relax into a state of sweet dreams with this rest-time wand. To make one cut out two identical star shapes from tagboard. Brush one side of each star with glue; then sprinkle it with glitter. When the glue is dry, glue the stars together glitter sides out, leaving an opening in the bottom. Hot-glue an unsharpened pencil in the opening. During rest time use the wand to sprinkle imaginary pixie dust over the heads of your youngsters. Pleasant dreams!

Kristen Sharpe—Preschool
Kristen's Corner
Mansfield, MA

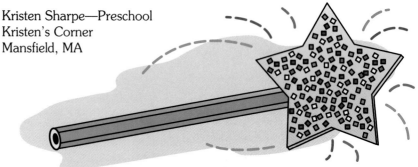

Easy Dismissal

This parent-friendly dismissal routine gives you a chance to say good-bye to each child individually. Write each child's name on a separate index card. Just before dismissal time, place the cards outside your classroom door. When a parent arrives, he slips his child's name card under the door. Quietly help that child gather her things; then deliver her to the parent. Should a parent need to speak to you, suggest that he remain until all of the children have been dismissed.

Joan Banker—Four-Year-Olds
St. Mary's Child Development Center
Garner, NC

In A Row
Tips For Getting Organized

Match Mates

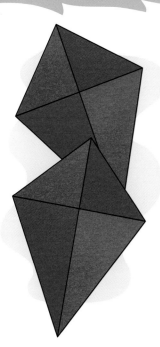

Here's a management tip for seating at snacktimes and circle times that doubles as an opportunity to reinforce visual-discrimination skills. Prepare matching pairs of shapes for various seasons, holidays, and themes. For example, cut pairs of mitten shapes from wallpaper patterns, or similarly decorate pairs of heart cutouts. To use the match mates during a group time, place one shape in a matching pair at a seat or on the floor in your group area. Give the matching shape to a child. Direct each child to find his spot by finding his matching shape.

Susan Burbridge—Four-Year-Olds
Trinity Weekday School
San Antonio, TX

Field-Trip Tip

Here's a tip that will keep your youngsters entertained on bus rides. For each child tie a lacing yarn through one of a lacing shape's holes. As each student boards the bus, hand him a shape. Encourage each child to complete his shape, then exchange it with a friend. No more boring bus rides!

Karen Saner
Burns Elementary School

All Is Fair

If you have an Easter-egg hunt at your preschool, here is an easy way to make sure each child finds her fair share of the goodies. Have each child paint and decorate an egg carton (or egg-carton half). During the hunt direct each child to fill her carton with eggs. When her carton is full, she may leave the hunt to admire her findings while other children continue to search. Everyone is sure to have her fair share of fun!

Diane Lundgren—Preschool
One Step Ahead Home Preschool
Columbia, MO

Getting Your Ducklings

Nifty Nametags

Your little ones will be happy to lend you a hand when making these self-adhering nametags for your tables or cubbies. To make a nametag, cut a square of clear Con-Tact® covering that is slightly larger than a child's hand. Remove the backing from the square. Have a child press his hand into tempera paint, then onto the adhesive side of the Con-Tact® covering. When the paint is dry, press the square onto a tabletop or the child's cubby; then use a permanent marker to write the child's name below his handprint. What a nifty nametag!

Carolyn Macdonald—
    Four-Year-Olds
Kiddie Haven Day Care
Brockton, MA

Lori

Snappy Center Management

Youngsters will independently choose and change learning centers with this photographic management system. Take an individual photo of each child and each of your classroom centers. Mount each picture onto a same-sized piece of cardboard. Cover each mounted photo with clear Con-Tact® covering; then attach a piece of magnetic tape to the back of it. Use masking tape to visually divide a magnetic surface into a grid with enough spaces for each center's photo and the number of children you will allow in that center at one time. Arrange the pictures of the centers on the grid. When choosing a center, a child places her picture in a space next to her chosen

center's photo. When all the spaces are filled, the center is full.

Christine Zieleniewski—Pre-K, Saint Cecilia School, Kearny, NJ

Stick 'em Up!

Tired of rolling tape in order to adhere calendar markers to your calendar? Try this sticky tip! Laminate your calendar, daily markers, and an extra sheet of poster board. Squeeze a drop of Aleene's™ Tack-It over & over glue onto the back of each marker. Allow the glue to dry. Stick the markers on the extra sheet of poster board to store them. During your calendar time, stick the day's marker on your calendar. These pieces will stick to your calendar over and over again!

Judy Kuhn Skaggs—Three-Year-Olds, Highland Preschool, Raleigh, NC

In A Row
Tips For Getting Organized

Here's The Ticket

Looking for a way to organize your learning center time? If so, then this idea may be just the ticket you need! Request that a home-supplies store donate countertop samples that are no longer in use. To make a ticket for each child, trim his picture; then tape it onto a sample. Personalize the tickets. In each of your classroom centers, screw as many cup hooks into a wooden surface as you will allow children in that center at one time. Store the tickets near your group area. To choose a center, a child hangs his ticket on one of the center's hooks.

Sam

Nicky Daigle— Non-Categorical Preschool
Thibodaux Elementary
Thibodaux, LA

Beautiful Bulletin Boards

Your bulletin boards will look appealing all year long when you back them with neutral-colored wallpaper before adding your display pieces. Wallpaper is durable, and its color won't fade. With this method you'll save time, and your bulletin boards will look great display after display.

Susan Dzurovcik—Preschool
Valley Road School
Clark, NJ

Rebus Calendar

Use this rebus calendar to help your preschoolers remember on which days they attend special classes or activities. On separate cards or sentence-strip lengths, write each of the days your class attends school and each of your weekly classes and activities, such as art and music. Draw a picture of each of your weekly classes on separate cards or use photos to represent each activity. To prepare the calendar, display the labels of the days, the pictures of the activities, and the activity labels on a chart or pocket chart as shown. Use an arrow cutout or other symbol to point to the current day. Replace the pictures and labels as needed to include field trips, parties, or other special events.

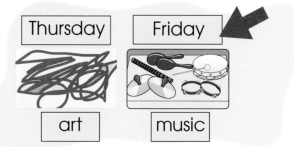

Mary Jenks—Preschool, Special Education (Hearing Impaired)
Briarlake Elementary
Decatur, GA

161

Roly-Poly Portraits

Prepare these picture cubes and you'll roll right into games and transitions! Obtain a plastic picture cube for every six children in your class. Personalize a photo of each child. Insert a different child's photo into each side of each cube. (As an alternative, glue photos to the sides of empty mug gift boxes.) Use the picture cubes to work on classmate recognition or name recognition. Or roll the cubes to assign jobs and centers. When playing games, roll the cube to determine whose turn it is. With these ideas, you're on a roll!

Ginette M. Harvey and Traci Kilbreath—Three-, Four-, And Five-Year-Olds
Portage County Integrated Preschool, Aurora, OH

Lovely Labels

When you use this easy tip for making picture labels for containers and shelves, children will know at a glance where everything belongs! Make a color or black-and-white photocopy of each item to be stored or shelved. Cut out the pictures; then use clear Con-Tact® covering to attach them to the appropriate shelves or containers. During cleanup times, students can refer to the pictures in order to replace materials easily.

Mandi King—Pre-K
Hubbard Pre-K
Forsyth, GA

Zipper Chair

Do your little ones need an easy way to get help with their coat zippers? Try this adorable idea. Use fabric paint to paint a zipper on the front of a T-shirt. When the paint is dry, put the shirt over the back of a chair. (As an alternative, place a real coat with a zipper on the chair back.) Label the seat "Zipper Chair," and then cover the label with clear Con-Tact® covering. Next place the chair near your closet or the door. Encourage students to sit in the Zipper Chair when they encounter difficulty zipping up their jackets and coats to go outside. Or have a seat in the Zipper Chair and invite those children who need help to come to you. Zip 'em up and take 'em out!

Terry Steinke—Preschool
Emmaus Lutheran School, Indianapolis, IN

Your little farmhands are sure to crow over this barnyard display. Staple bandanas to a bulletin board. Prepare a large tagboard barn cutout; then cut a number of windows out of the barn. Take full-length pictures of your students; then cut the developed pictures around each child's body shape. Tape some of the pictures behind the windows. Mount the barn on the background; then arrange the remaining photos on the display.

Diann Kroos—Infants To Three-Year-Olds
Donald O. Clifton Child Development Center
Lincoln, NE

This progressive display reflects a year's worth of learning activities and themes. Use various colors of bulletin-board-paper lengths to divide a wall into as many sections as there are months in your school year. Label the sections with the names of the months. Fill each section with photos and student work from that month's theme or learning activities. As you add to the display, children will see the progression of time, and parents will see the progression of learning!

Darlene V. Martino—Pre-K, Palmyra Head Start, Palmyra, NY

This helper train will keep you on track when assigning classroom jobs. Cut simple shapes from tagboard to create a train. (Make sure the engine and cars together equal the number of classroom jobs you will have.) Label the engine and cars with different jobs. Mount the train on a scenic background. Assign classroom jobs by taping children's laminated photos to the engine and boxcars.

Amanda M. Brown—Three-Year-Olds, A Child's View, Newton, NC

This door display is the pick of the crop for welcoming preschoolers! Cover the door with paper; then add a border of apple cutouts. On a large apple cutout labeled "Welcome," glue large pom-poms and a pair of wiggle eyes to resemble a worm. Add the apple to the door along with students' personalized, sponge-painted apple cutouts. What an appealing door display!

adapted from an idea by Alicia Mia
  Dillingham—Pre-K
Denbigh Early Childhood Center
Newport News, VA

Pre-K Is Harvesting Fall Fun!

Gather your youngsters to help you make this display. Mount a bulletin-board-paper tree; then adorn it with students' sponge-painted leaf shapes. Have students glue orange and black tissue-paper pieces to paper plates to make a patch of jack-o'-lanterns; then pile the smiling pumpkins beneath the tree. You're really harvesting now!

Laura Fitz—Pre-K, Baltimore County Public School, Baltimore, MD

This display lets everyone know that you really give a hoot who's present each day! Mount a paper tree so that the branches are within students' reach. Enlarge and color an owl character; then mount it on the tree along with a caption. Mount a laminated basket shape below the tree. Each season, use Sticky-Tac to attach personalized, laminated shapes—such as apples, leaves, snowflakes, or birds—to the basket. Ask children to attach their shapes to the branches as they arrive each day.

Karen Eiben—Three-Year-Olds
The Kids' Place
LaSalle, IL

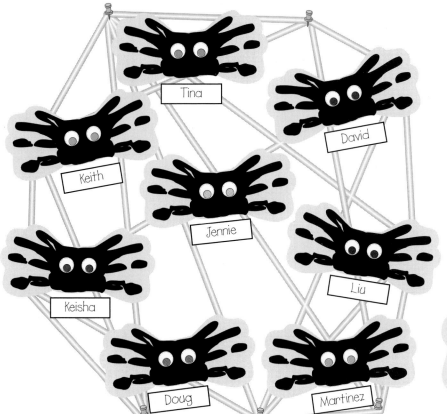

Feeling creepy? Use pushpins and glittery yarn to create a web on a wall. Then fill the web with a handful of spiders. To make a spider, direct a child to dip both hands into black paint, then press them onto paper. When the paint is dry, cut around the shape, removing the thumbprints. Glue on wiggle eyes before adding the "creepy-crawly" and the child's name to the display.

Jennifer Liptak—Pre-K
Sonshine Preschool
Bensalem, PA

Watch out for compliments with this "color-fall" bulletin board. Post a sign on a background; then enlarge and color a character to add to the board. Surround the critter with student-painted watercolor leaves. If desired, add real leaves to the falling foliage.

Cathy Overton—Toddlers & Three-Year-Olds, St. Andrew's Preschool, Nags Head, NC

BULLETIN BOARDS

"Tree-mendous" Accomplishments

Students adorn this Christmas tree with decorations as they achieve group goals, such as cleaning cooperatively or eating politely at snacktime. Each time you would like to praise your group, note their accomplishment on a paper shape. Then ask a volunteer to mount the shape on the tree. Your star students are sure to shine with pride!

We cleaned our centers quietly.

Use your little ones' artwork to create either of these holiday displays. Invite each child to paint or color on a white construction-paper circle. Glue each circle onto a larger yellow circle for a Hanukkah display or green circle for a Christmas display. Trim the larger circles with pinking shears. Mount these projects in the desired shape. Happy holidays!

Friends Work Together

We can share crayons.

We are building a tower.

We can help clean up.

We can do the puzzle together.

Enlarge a set of friendly characters for this bulletin board that encourages cooperation and friendship. Mount the characters on a background. Then, as you see children working together, take an instant photo. On construction paper, write the students' description of their activity. Add the picture and the statement to the display. Friends work together!

Laura McDonough—Integrated Special Education Preschool, Brightwood Elementary School, Springfield, MA

Reluctant to put away your class Christmas tree? Remove the holiday ornaments and replace them with ornaments that emphasize the letters of the alphabet. Using a die cutter and simple patterns, make an ornament for each letter. Have students help you decorate the tree, or add an ornament to the tree each time you focus your studies on a different letter. Top the tree with a paper rainbow.

Sharon Sinn—Pre-K
IACC Daycare Center
Ithaca, NY

ALPHABET TREE

We're As Sweet As Candy!

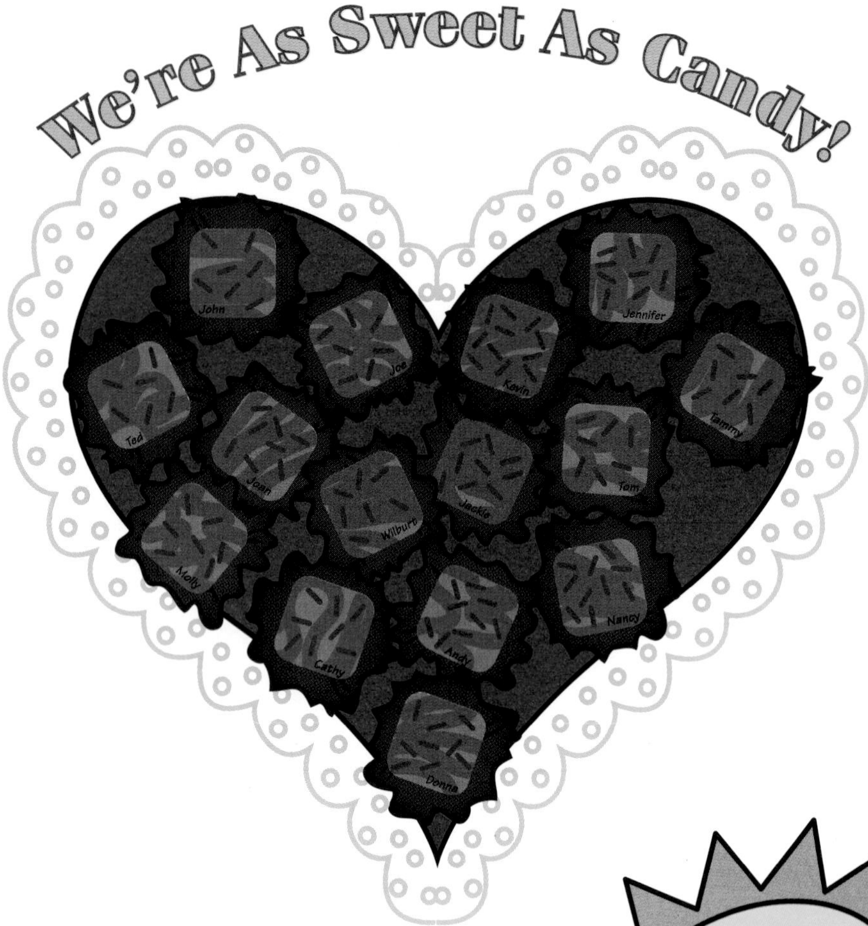

This display is as sweet as can be! Glue lace trim to a large, red heart shape; then mount the heart and a title on a wall. To make delicious-looking chocolates, provide each child with a personalized, tan construction-paper shape. Have him paint his paper with brown tempera paint and top it with real chocolate sprinkles. When each shape is dry, glue it to a larger piece of crinkled black paper to represent the candy wrapper. Mount the finished projects on the heart.

Brandi Kimball—One-, Two-, And Three-Year-Olds
Growing Years, Inc.
Basalt, CO

Faith and begorra! With this door display, your children will walk right under a rainbow! Hang varying lengths and colors of crepe-paper streamers from the top of your classroom door frame. Mount a sun cutout above the door; then add a large, cloud-shaped cutout atop the streamers' ends to complete the dazzling display.

Cindy Goodrich
Forestbrook Elementary School
Myrtle Beach, SC

Celebrate your youngsters' growing skills with this floral display! To prepare, snap a photo of each child engaged in a different classroom activity. Mount each child's photo on a paper plate. Write his dictated sentence about his abilities (as shown in the picture) on the plate. Then invite him to create a construction-paper flower using the paper plate as its center. Add green crepe-paper stems to the flowers; then mount them on a bulletin board, along with the title "Growing Up!"

Cheryl Gibson—Pre-K, Sedgefield Elementary, Greensboro, NC

Tell the world what a lucky teacher you are with this St. Patrick's Day door display! Mount a black posterboard pot on the corner of your door. Invite each child to decorate a yellow construction-paper circle with his choice of glimmering gold items, such as glitter, pipe cleaners, sequins, beads, and foil wrapping paper. Title your door. Then mount the golden circles on the door as if they are pouring out of the pot. Finally, add each child's name on a bright piece of construction paper near his gold piece.

BULLETIN BOARDS

"CHICK" IT OUT!

Spring Picnic

This Week!

Help Needed:

Use this clever display to get parents to take a peek at your current classroom events. At one end of a hallway, mount two halves of a large, cracked poster-board egg; then fill the remaining hall space with chick projects. To make each chick, use brads to attach a student's cut-out hand shapes to a paper egg shape; then add paper feet, eyes, and a beak along with feathers, if desired. Add to the display current announcements or pictures of your spring activities.

Help each child use different colors of bingo markers to create a pattern on a paper egg shape. Next fringe one side of a length of green bulletin-board paper to resemble grass. Staple the length on a display to create a pocket. Add more grass pockets, if desired. Tuck the decorated eggs in the grass; then put a real basket near the display. To use, a child takes an egg out of the grass. He then identifies the pattern before putting the egg in the basket.

adapted from an idea by Betsy Ruggiano—Preschool
Featherbed Lane School
Clark, NJ

Hunting For Patterns

AND DISPLAYS

Moms will grin with delight at this board and be tickled, too, with the take-home treats! For each child, prepare a head-and-shoulders outline on poster board. Encourage each child to use markers to illustrate the outline to represent his mom. Label the project. Then provide each child with a length of yarn and decorative beads for making a necklace. Punch two holes through the poster board at the shoulders. Thread the necklace through the holes; then tie the ends together at the back. Display the projects and watch for smiles.

Nancy Segars—Four-Year-Olds, First Baptist Preschool, Lawrenceville, GA

Our Classroom Bouquet

Each child contributes to this giant display in a big way! Precut a circle in the center of a paper plate for each child; then personalize the plate. Have each child glue paper petals, a stem, and leaves to the plate. Tape the child's picture to the back of the plate. Arrange the flowers on a wall along with a bulletin-board-paper pot. Add a class photo to the pot and a title to the display.

Theresa Reth—Four-Year-Olds, Little People's College, New Bedford, MA

You've Come A Long Way, Baby!

My feet and hands are big now!
Terry

I have lots of teeth in my smile.
Lorna

I don't have little fingers anymore.
Steve

My hair is darker now.
Julie

My hair grew. I was bald.
Gracie

I have gotten very tall.
Annette

I can run fast now!
Kara

Ask each child to bring a baby picture to school. Mount the photo on a colorful piece of paper along with a recent picture taken at school. On the paper, write as each child describes how he has grown. Share the pictures with the group before mounting them on a wall or bulletin board.

Michelle Castonguay—Preschool, Someplace Special Preschool, Holyoke, MA

Take A Bite Out Of Summer!

I'm going to Grandma's.

I'm going to play in Britt's yard.

I will play with my cousins.

I'll be jumping in my pool.

Sarah Francis will come play.

My sister and I are going to visit my Auntie.

My daddy is taking me on a trip.

No matter how you slice them, these watermelons make a luscious display. When each child has enjoyed a slice of real watermelon, have him wash and dry the seeds. Have him glue a pink half-circle to a slightly larger green half-circle; then glue the real seeds onto the paper slice. Write on his watermelon slice as each child dictates his summer plans. Before attaching it to a background, tear a bite out of the slice. Add paper vines and a title to complete the display.

Andrea Esposito—Preschool, VA/YMCA Child Care Center, Brooklyn, NY

AND DISPLAYS

Sailing Off To Kindergarten

Ahoy, teachers of four-year-olds! Here's a display just for you! Mount blue plastic wrap onto a blue background. Add a title along with sun and cloud cutouts. Take pictures of your youngsters in various poses; then cut the developed pictures around each child's body shape. Arrange the photos on construction-paper boats; then add them to your scene. Set the sails for a terrific display!

Eleanore Cirigliano—Preschool, KidsPort Learning Center, Plymouth, MA

Have your crew help you prepare this whale of an ocean mural. To create the ocean floor, paint glue onto scalloped lengths of tan paper; then sprinkle on a mixture of dried beans. Later mount the lengths onto a blue background. Cut whale shapes (pattern on page 176) from papers that have been fingerpainted blue, black, and white. Add a wiggle eye to each whale; then display the whales on the background.

Nancy Perkins—Pre-K, Itty Bitty Preschool, Glendale, AZ

Whale Pattern

Use with the display on page 175.

OUR
READERS
WRITE

Our Readers Write

Clown Greeter

Help youngsters find their classroom by sitting a cheerful clown greeter by the door. To make the clown's head, use fiberfill to stuff a cut-off panty-hose leg. Tie the open end of the panty-hose; then attach a colorful clown wig and construction-paper facial features to it. Attach a red foam ball or small inflated balloon to serve as the nose. To make the body, stuff a clown costume and attach the head at the neck of the costume. Attach a stuffed glove to the end of each sleeve and a glittery tennis shoe to the end of each pant leg. As a final touch, place a large, tissue-paper flower on the clown's head to serve as a hat. Position the clown in a chair outside your classroom door. Children will proudly greet the clown as they independently find their own classroom each day.

Melissa Epling—Preschool
Panther Creek Preschool
Nettie, WV

Customized Labels

Add a special touch to youngsters' school-made projects with customized labels. Have an inexpensive order of labels printed to read "I made this in [name of school and grade]," or "I made this with [name of teacher]." As each child completes a project, attach one of the special labels to it to serve as a memento.

Chava Shapiro
Beth Rochel School
Monsey, NY

> I Made This In
> Beth Rochel
> Preschool

Good-Morning Aprons

Greet each child personally with this neat apron idea. Purchase or make an apron for each child. Print his name on the apron using a permanent marker or fabric paint. During a morning group time, hold up one apron at a time so the children can see the name on it. As each child recognizes his own name, have him raise his hand and greet you. Return the child's greeting; then place the apron on him. With these aprons, not only does each child receive a personal greeting, but he's prepared to tackle any messy activities that await him!

Rebecca A. Rush—Special Education, Mt. Pleasant Elementary, Claymont, DE

Looking Glasses

Are you looking for a different way to help youngsters focus their attention? Well, look no more! This great glasses idea will keep your little ones' sights fixed on the task at hand. For each child, purchase a pair of inexpensive children's sunglasses. Remove the lenses from the frame. Provide each child with a pair of these looking glasses to wear as they tour the school or meet school personnel. Then use the glasses throughout the year for activities such as looking for a particular teacher on her birthday, examining items in the science center, looking for trash on the playground–or anytime as an extra incentive to maintain students' attention.

Sue Lewis Lein—Four-Year-Olds
St. Pius X
Wauwatosa, WI

Follow The Streamer

Little ones will soon be finding their own way around the classroom with this streamer idea. On the lower portion of a wall outside your classroom, post a nametag for each child. Attach the end of a streamer to each child's nametag; then attach the other end of the streamer to the child's cubby. As each child arrives on the first day, encourage him to find his nametag, then follow the attached streamer into the room to locate his cubby. Within the classroom, have students follow streamers that attach their cubbies to particular centers, or that attach one center to another. By simply following the streamers, youngsters will independently transition from one area of the room to another!

Amy Barsanti—Pre-K, St. Andrew's Preschool, Nags Head, NC

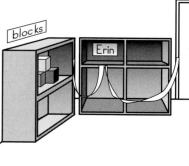

Artistic Names

Youngsters will be delighted to see their personalized name strips displayed on a class welcome board! Using block-style stencil letters, trace each child's name onto a strip of art paper. Have each child decorate the letters in his name using a variety of art mediums such as paint, crayons, and markers. Invite the children to help arrange the decorated name strips on a welcome-board display.

Melinda Davidson—Preschool/Integrated Special Needs
Brockton Early Childhood Program
Brockton, MA

Window Murals

Do you have a large window in your classroom that needs to be livened up? If so, paint a mural on it. To make a mural, use washable markers to draw a seasonal scene or some characters on the window. Mix a small amount of dishwashing liquid with different colors of washable paint. If the students can easily reach the window, have them paint the mural. When it dries, use the mural as a topic for discussion or encourage youngsters to add their own related artwork to it. When you are ready to remove or replace the mural, simply wash the paint off the window.

Kim Richman—Two- And Three-Year-Olds
The Learning Zone
Des Moines, IA

Inexpensive Party Supplies

Invite youngsters to help you prepare some of these easy, inexpensive decorations for classroom celebrations. To make a decorative tablecloth, cut a piece of butcher paper slightly larger than a tabletop. Have students sponge-paint designs related to the celebration theme on the paper. Invite children to decorate solid-colored cups and napkins with theme-related stickers. To create treat bags, have the children put stickers on plastic sandwich bags. With these ideas, celebration preparations will be just as much fun as the celebration!

Janine Nordland—Four- And Five-Year-Olds, Kids' Korner, Owatonna, MN

Name Cards

Make these multiple-use name cards to help your students recognize their own and their classmate's names. Print each child's name on a separate index card. To provide each child with numerous exposures to her name, use the name cards for activities such as lining up, grouping students for centers, and playing games that require taking turns. When the students are familiar with their first names in print, write each student's last name on the back of her name card.

Elaine Swindell—Preschool, Providence Preschool, Swan Quarter, NC

Name Match Game

Use these matching games to give students practice in sequencing the letters in their names. To make a game, write a child's name on a length of sentence strip. Write each letter in the child's name on a separate 2 1/2" length of sentence strip. Attach a piece of adhesive-backed magnetic tape to the back of each piece. To play, have a child place his name strip on a magnetic board. Encourage him to sequence the letter strips on the board to correctly spell his name, referring to the name strip as necessary. Store each child's name and letter strips in a resealable plastic storage bag.

Jane Hall—Four-Year-Olds
Trinity Church Day School
Long Green, MD

Easy Blender Applesauce

Invite youngsters to take advantage of a harvest-time favorite when they help make this applesauce recipe.

Applesauce

6 large apples
3/4 cup water
sugar to taste
cinnamon to taste

Peel, core, and cut the apples into chunks. Put the water and a few chunks of apple in a blender. Blend the mixture, adding the remaining apple chunks a few at a time until the mixture becomes soft. Add sugar and cinnamon to taste and mix well. Serve the applesauce to each student in a small paper cup. This recipe makes approximately three cups of applesauce.

Linda Lopienski
Asheboro, NC

Our Readers Write

Cap Counting

There's no cap on the amount of counting fun your little ones will have with these games. Program each strip in a supply of black construction-paper strips with an orange paper numeral; then add the corresponding number of orange paper circles to each strip. Laminate the strips. Use a permanent black marker to draw jack-o'-lantern faces on a supply of orange jug lids. To use these materials, a child counts as he puts the appropriate number of lids on each strip.

Similarly make Christmas-themed counting games by programming construction-paper tree cutouts with numerals and circles. Provide various colors of jug lids to represent ornaments.

Sharron Coletta—Three-Year-Olds
Chamblee-Methodist Kindergarten
Chamblee, GA

Marbleized Pumpkin

If you're looking for an age-appropriate art activity, pick this pumpkin idea. To make one pumpkin, trace a circular cake pan onto white or orange paper; then cut along the resulting outline. Next put the paper cutout in the pan. After dipping a marble in orange tempera paint, drop it into the pan and keep it rolling. Remove the paper from the pan. When the paint is dry, complete the project by gluing on construction-paper facial features and a stem.

Cheryl Songer—Preschool
Wee Know Nursery School
Wales, WI

The Family Tree

Invite your children's families to help you keep this year-round display decorated. Mount a large paper tree in a hallway or on a bulletin board near your school's entrance. Every month, provide each child's family with a seasonal construction-paper shape to creatively decorate. Arrange these projects on the tree's branches. Look what's on the family tree this month!

Suzi Dodson—Preschool
Growing Years Early Learning Center
Claysburg, PA

Painting Tip

Painting a lunch bag to make a pumpkin or puppet is easy when you insert an empty, rectangular tissue box into the bag. The box makes the bag easier to manipulate and easier to paint on all four sides. It also keeps the bag upright while it is drying.

Linda Gilligan—Pre-K
St. Hedwig School
Naugatuck, CT

Eight-Legged Pretzels

These savory spiders are easy to make and quick to bake. If desired, have your students help you mix up a batch of bread dough, or save time by using refrigerated dough. To make a pretzel, crisscross four dough lengths atop one another on a piece of aluminum foil. Press a dough ball on top of the lengths; then sprinkle the spider with kosher salt. Bake, cool, and then munch!

Lori Kracoff—Preschool
The Curious George Cottage Learning Center
Waterville Valley, NH

Yarn-Painted Border

Turn an age-appropriate art activity into a beautiful bulletin-board border. Provide youngsters with sheets of bulletin-board paper, shallow trays of tempera paint, and lengths of yarn. Invite each of your little ones to dip a length of yarn into the paint, then drag it across the paper to create a design. When the paint has dried, cut the paper into equal-width strips. Add an interesting scalloped or zigzag edge to each strip, if desired, before attaching the border to a bulletin board. Your preschool painters will be so proud!

Karen Bryant—Pre-K
Miller Elementary School, Warner Robins, GA

X Rays

During a unit on health or body awareness, take an imaginary X ray of each child's arm and hand. If possible, show the children a real X ray. Explain that when a real X ray is taken, the patient must wear an apron. Then ask each child, in turn, to don an apron for her imaginary X ray. Have the child press her hand and arm into a shallow tray of white tempera paint, then onto a sheet of black construction paper. Use a white crayon or colored pencil to label each child's X ray with her name and the date. Send each X ray home as a preschool memento.

Brenda vonSeldeneck and
  Donna Selling—Preschool
First Presbyterian Church
Waynesboro, VA

Nate Williams   October, 1996

Mystery And Discover

Add a little excitement to your center time! Create two new centers for your youngsters to visit—Mystery and Discover. At a Mystery center, encourage youngsters to explore and create with a new, previously untried set of manipulatives. At a Discovery center, place any bright, attractive, unusual gadget you can find, along with magnifying glasses, a microscope, measuring tapes, pencils, and paper. Invite little ones to discover all they can about the object and record their findings.

Dawn Moore, Mt. View Elementary, Thorndike, ME

Halloween Costumes All Year Long

Dressing up is fun all year long—not just at Halloween! Take advantage of sales on Halloween costumes just before and just after the holiday to build a collection of costumes for your dramatic-play area. You might also send a note to each child's family prior to Halloween, requesting that used costumes be donated to the class after the holiday is over. If desired, specify the types of costumes you are interested in for the classroom.

Jill McClain—Preschool, Grand Rapids, MI

Glue Boo

There's not a ghost of a chance that your little ones will boo this Halloween handicraft! To make a ghost necklace, invite each youngster to squeeze the outline shape of a ghost onto a scrap piece of laminating film. Have her fill the outline completely with glue. Allow the glue to dry overnight; then peel it off the laminating film. Encourage each child to use a permanent marker to draw a face on her ghost. Punch a hole at the top and thread the pendant onto a length of orange or black yarn. Goodness gracious—what gorgeous ghosts!

Jeanne Puyau—Three-
  And Four-Year-Olds
Julius Rosenwald Elementary
New Orleans, LA

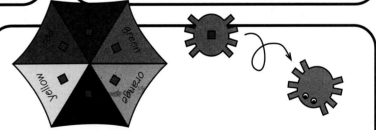

Creepy-Crawly Color Game

Use some paper spiders and their web to create a color-matching activity. First make a playing board by cutting a six-sided, spiderweb shape from white poster board. Draw lines to divide the web into six equal-sized, pie-shaped sections. Color each section a different color; then print the corresponding color word on the outer edge of each section. Cut six spiders from black construction paper; then hole-punch a pair of eyes for each spider that corresponds to a color on the playing board. Glue a pair of eyes to each spider. Finish assembling the game by affixing one piece of adhesive magnetic tape to each section of the playing board and one to the back of each spider. To play, a child matches each spider's eye color to the corresponding color on the web playing board.

Niki Huff—Pre-K, Stilwell United Methodist Preschool, Stilwell, KS

Our Readers Write

Magical Menorah

Have your class help make this menorah display this Hanukkah season. Gather eight toilet-tissue-paper tubes, one paper-towel tube, and one gift-wrap tube. Hot-glue a piece of cardboard to the bottom of the gift-wrap tube to make a base. Use an X-acto® knife to cut in the gift-wrap tube nine openings the same diameter as the remaining tubes. Insert the remaining tubes. Paint the menorah. On the first day of Hanukkah, insert a tissue-paper square into the top of the center tube and into one toilet-tissue tube to represent flames. "Light" one more candle with a tissue-paper flame on each of the remaining days of Hanukkah.

Ellen S. Farina—Preschool
Fort Lauderdale Prep School
Ft. Lauderdale, FL

"Toy-rific" Tree

Looking for a fun way to decorate your classroom Christmas tree? If so, then look no further than the toys on your classroom shelves. Simply string beads or connect Learning Links® to make colorful garlands. Twist pipe cleaners around toy animals, DUPLO® people, bear counters, or other small manipulatives. Then hang the items on the tree. Place a star-shaped manipulative on the top for a tree that's totally "toy-rific"!

Amy Deml—Preschool
Mary Of Lourdes Community Preschool
Little Falls, MN

Smells Like Christmas

The recipient of this ornament is sure to enjoy its delightful holiday scent! To make one, remove the double-sided tape from the back of a holiday-scented stick ups® air freshener. Twist open the air freshener; then thread a pipe cleaner through the top. Twist the ends together to create a loop. Decorate the air freshener with a variety of craft supplies, such as beads, glitter, buttons, sequins, and stickers.

Charlet Keller—Preschool
ICC Preschool
Violet Hill, AR

Gift Bags

Your little elves will love making these gift bags for holding gifts. To make one, glue a tree cutout to one side of a paper bag. Decorate the tree with painted, seasonally shaped pasta pieces and a foil star. After placing a gift in the bag, punch two holes through the top of the bag. Lace a length of ribbon through the holes; then thread a small gift card onto the ribbon. Tie the ribbon into a bow. Youngsters will be pleased as punch to take home these pretty presents!

Jackie Wright—Preschool And Gr. K
Summerhill Children's House, Enid, OK

Merry Christmas To Sarah

Handsome Gift Wrap

This easy gift wrap is sure to be a hands-down favorite with your youngsters. Invite each child to create his own gift wrap by repeatedly pressing a hand in paint, then onto a sheet of tissue paper or bulletin-board paper. When the paint is dry, assist him in using his paper to wrap a special gift.

Donna Leonard—Preschool, Head Start, Dyersville, IA

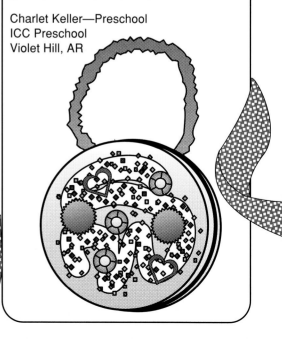

Christmas Countdown

With this countdown calendar, Santa's beard will be soft and fluffy just in time for Christmas Day! Look where party supplies are sold for holiday plates that display Santa's face. On each of a class supply of plates, write the numerals 1–24 on Santa's beard. For each child, place a programmed plate and 24 cotton balls in a resealable plastic bag. Attach the following poem to each bag; then send home the items on the first day of December.

Dayle Timmons—Special Education Pre-K
Alimacani Elementary School
Jacksonville, FL

How many days till
    Christmas?
Let me help you count.
Let's add one cotton ball
    each day;
There's just the right
    amount.

And when Santa's beard
Is full and soft and white,
Go to sleep very early,
'Cause Santa comes
    this night!

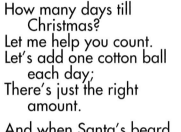

Happy "Holly-days"!

Dress your classroom in Christmas cheer with these "holly-day" prints! Cut several holly shapes from sponges. Invite each child to dip a sponge into green paint, then press it onto a large sheet of construction paper. Next have him use a red sponge-tipped bingo marker to paint berries. Deck your walls with prints of holly. Fa-la-la-la-la, la-la-la-la!

Dayle Timmons

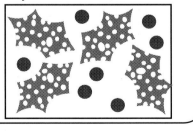

Problem Solved

If you have wooden puzzles that have too many pieces for your little ones to solve, try this terrific tip. Glue several small pieces of a puzzle together to make one large piece. Now with bigger pieces, even difficult puzzles are easy to solve.

Susan Sykes—Preschool
Denbigh Early Childhood Center, Hampton, VA

Craft Wrap

Use inexpensive wrapping paper with big designs to improve your little ones' cutting skills. Stock a center with gift wrap, construction paper, scissors, and glue. Invite a student to cut out the designs on the gift wrap, then glue them onto construction paper. Students will be delighted with the endless creative possibilities these patterns supply!

Jackie Wright—Preschool And Gr. K
Summerhill Children's House, Enid, OK

Better Borders

Add some gift-wrap glitz to your bulletin boards with this nifty idea. Cut lengths of seasonal or thematic wrapping paper into three-inch-wide strips. Laminate the strips for durability; then staple them around a bulletin-board display. For extra pizzazz, coordinate your borders and titles by cutting out letters from matching paper. Beautiful!

Cindy S. Berry—Two-Year-Olds
Christian Kindergarten And Nursery School
Little Rock, AR

Magic Reindeer Mix

The bright light from Rudolph's nose is sure to help him find this magical reindeer mix! Mix some gold glitter into a container of dry oatmeal. Invite each child to scoop some reindeer mix into a personalized plastic sandwich bag. Attach a copy of the following note to each bag. Your little ones are sure to hear the pitter-patter of reindeer hooves racing to gobble up this tasty treat!

Kay Mayberry—Preschool
Good Shepherd Learning Center
Lafayette, IN

On Christmas Eve before you go to bed, sprinkle this magic reindeer food on your lawn. The magic glitter and the smell of the oats will help guide Rudolph to your house!

Magic Eyes Matrix

Little ones will be delighted to use their "magic eyes" to discover the hidden pictures on this matrix. To prepare the matrix, draw a three-column grid of equal-sized boxes on a sheet of poster board. Select a theme, such as a holiday, or a topic such as bears. Duplicate, color, and cut out six copies of as many different pictures as you have rows on your matrix. Across each row, glue one picture in the first box, two pictures in the second box, and three pictures in the third box as shown. Cut a piece of tagboard the size of one box on the matrix to use as a screen. Discuss the chart with the class, leading youngsters to understand the relationship between the columns and rows. Then cover a box with the screen. Ask youngsters to use their "magic eyes" to examine the matrix to "see" the hidden pictures.

Judy Aronson—Integrated Preschool
Salem Early Childhood Center, Bentley School
Salem, MA

Snowy Science

Let it snow and you'll have a super science lesson that only takes minutes to prepare. At the start of a snowy school day, fill a fishbowl with lightly packed snow. Set the bowl in your science center; then place a small toy sailboat atop the snow. Encourage youngsters to observe and comment on the changes that take place during the day as the snow melts and the boat begins to float.

Sharon Patterson—Four-Year-Olds, Littlestown Christian Academy
Littlestown, PA

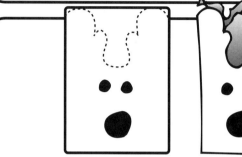

Rudolph Gift Bag

Rudolph with his nose so bright, makes a gift bag look just right! To make a reindeer gift bag, trace an antlers shape onto the top of a flattened brown paper lunch bag. Cut along the lines; then use markers to add eyes and a nose. Open the bag; then tuck a sheet of colorful tissue paper inside. Fill the bag with hot-chocolate packets, dry cookie ingredients, or a student-made gift.

Jean M. Long—Preschool, Heart Of The Lake Schools, Perham, MN

Inexpensive Holiday Puzzles

Keep an eye out for inexpensive cardboard decorations this season; then buy double! To make a magnetic puzzle set, laminate each pair of decorations. Cut one of the decorations into several pieces. Attach self-adhesive magnetic tape to the back of each piece and to the whole decoration. To use the puzzle set, a student places the whole decoration on a magnet board, then places the pieces on the board to create a matching picture. What an inexpensive way to add to your classroom puzzle collection!

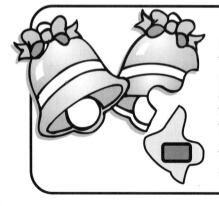

Tonie Northcutt—Preschool, Mother's Morning Out, Ancient City Baptist Church
St. Augustine, FL

Write And Wipe

Give students plenty of practice writing their first and last names. For each child, program a sentence strip by writing his first name on one side and his last name on the opposite side. Laminate all of the strips. Place the strips in a writing center along with wipe-off markers and Handi Wipes. Once a student traces and writes his name, have him wipe his work away and practice again another day.

Rita Confer—Preschool
Gazebo School, Summerville, SC

Watch That Amaryllis Grow!

An amaryllis bloom is sure to brighten your winter classroom. And because the plant grows about an inch a day, it's the perfect math and science project for preschoolers! Purchase your bulb at a home-and-garden store; then follow the package directions as your little ones assist you in planting the bulb. When the bulb sprouts, measure and record its growth each day. Beautiful!

Pat Smith—Pre-K, Bells Elementary, Bells, TX

Seasonal Dice

These seasonal dice are great for little hands and minds! Measure up 2 1/4 inches from the bottom of each of two empty, clean eight-ounce milk cartons. Cut off the tops and discard. Fit the carton bottoms together to make one cube. Cover the cube with Con-Tact® covering; then program the sides with seasonal stickers. Use the dice with favorite classroom games or along with seasonal erasers for a simple counting activity. Get ready to roll!

Amy Aloi—Four-Year-Olds
Prince Georges County Head Start
   Berkshire Elementary
Forestville, MD

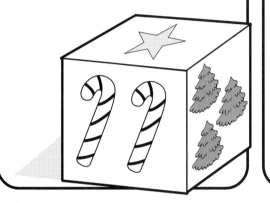

Money-Saving Border

Here's a pleasing patchwork bulletin-board border that will save you money! Cut wallpaper samples into three-inch-wide strips. Then staple the strips around your bulletin board for an inexpensive finishing touch.

Cindy S. Berry—Two-Year-Olds
Christian Kindergarten and Nursery School
Little Rock, AR

Button-Up Snowman

This frosty friend is ready to help your students sort. Collect three round, plastic lids that are graduated sizes (such as a yogurt-cup lid, a butter-tub lid, and a whipped-topping lid). Hot-glue the lids onto tagboard to resemble a snowman; then use permanent markers to add features. Supply a container of buttons. Encourage children to sort small buttons on the snowman's head, medium buttons on his middle, and large buttons on his base. Button up—it's cold outside!

Rhonda Monk—Preschool
Forest Hill Elementary School
Forest Hill, LA

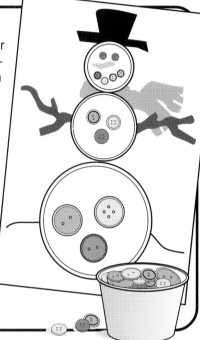

Holiday Manipulatives

Brighten up counting activities with some holiday sequins and your overhead projector. Invite your older preschoolers to work with these unique manipulatives in the following ways:

- Program each transparency in a set with a different numeral and corresponding dot set. Have a child place a transparency on the projector and cover each dot with a sequin. Ask her partner to count aloud the number of sequins projected onto the screen.
- Have a student place a plastic or die-cut numeral on the projector. Then have his partner place the correct number of sequins on the projector and count them with his buddy.
- Have a child make a pattern using the sequins on the projector. Have her partner read the pattern from the screen and continue the pattern.

Lorrie Hartnett, Canyon Lake, TX

Quik® Q Idea

Here is a quality center idea for teaching the letter Q. To prepare the center, locate a clean, empty box of Nestlé® Quik® chocolate milk mix. Next cut out a supply of drinking glass shapes from white tagboard. Color the bottom half of each glass brown to resemble chocolate milk. Program some of the glasses with the uppercase and lowercase letter Q, and the rest with other letters. To play the game, children look at the glasses and place only those with the letter Q into the Quik® box. Anybody thirsty for the letter Q?

Jill Beattie—Four- And Five-Year-Olds
Apple Place Nursery
Chambersburg, PA

Popcorn And Cranberry Ornaments

Shiny red cranberries team up with fluffy white popcorn to make these pretty ornaments. To make an ornament, thread popcorn and cranberries on midweight floral wire to create a simple pattern. When the wire is filled, bring the ends together, and then twist them to form a wreath. Hang these ornaments on a Christmas tree or outside your window so children can watch the birds feeding on them. The holidays truly are for everyone!

Jill Beattie—Four- And Five-Year-Olds

Our Readers Write

Storage Solution

Do you spend valuable time hunting for mis-placed materials? Then get organized with large, lidded card-board boxes (such as the ones used for copy paper or storage boxes). Label each box with the name of a theme that you teach, such as "Dinosaurs" or "Shapes." As you com-plete each unit, place all art samples, stories, flannelboard pieces, copies of fingerplays and songs, etc., inside the box. Storage will be a snap!

Cathy Schmidt—
    Three-, Four-, And
    Five-Year-Olds
De Pere Co-Op Nursery
    School
Green Bay, WI

A Wall Of Valentines

If you're looking for a way to extend the fun of a valentine-card exchange, try this decorative idea. Designate a section of a wall for each child, using name labels. Arrange pieces of rolled masking tape on the wall. After each child has opened his valentines, allow him to place his cards on the tape in his section to create a wall of valentines. Your children and their par-ents will enjoy this lovely display, and you can use it for counting and visual-discrimination games.

Andrea A. Esposito—Pre-K
VA/YMCA
Brooklyn, NY

Time To Spare?

Here's a colorful idea to help fill those few extra minutes between activities. Call out a color word. Have students walk quickly and place their hands on an item in the classroom that matches the color you called. Continue with other color words to fill the time as needed. On another day, vary the activity by calling out texture words.

Tracey Rebock—Pre-K
Temple Emanuel Preschool
Cherry Hill, NJ

Refrigerator Magnets

Here's a "hand-y" way to display art-work! Paint each child's hands with tempera paint and have her press handprints onto a sheet of tagboard. Cut out the handprints. Use a black marker to print the possessive form of the child's name on her left hand-print and the word "Artwork" on her right handprint. Attach pieces of magnetic tape to the backs of the cutouts. Present the magnets to par-ents as "hand-some" gifts for Valentine's Day!

Carmen Carpenter—Pre-K
Highland Preschool
Knightdale, NC

We Love Our Friends

Help children recognize classmates' names with this heart-shaped game. Cut a sheet of red poster board into a large heart shape. Glue a photo of each child in your class onto the cutout. Label each picture with the child's name. Cut small hearts from colored construction paper and print a child's name on each one. Allow children to match the names and pictures.

Kathy Rollins—Three- And Four-Year-Olds
Children's Creative Corner
Springfield, MA

Blooming Bouquets

These beautiful bouquets are a delightful gift for Valentine's Day. To make each flower, use an eyedropper to drop colored water onto a coffee filter. When the filter is dry, pinch and twist the center of it to form a bloom. Fold a green chenille stem in half. Twist the ends around the bloom for a stem; then secure it with green masking tape. Cut the tip off a paper snow-cone holder; then insert the flowers in the wide end to make a bouquet. Encourage each child to give her bouquet to someone special. Who wouldn't love getting these flowers?

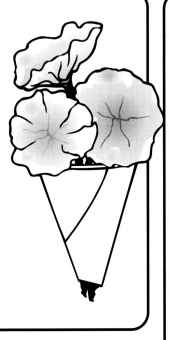

Linda Bille—Preschool
Riviera United Methodist Preschool
Redondo Beach, CA

A Printed Posy Valentine

Here's a pretty posy card made by printing with a bunch of celery! To make a card, fold a piece of construction paper; then glue a copy of the poem shown inside the card. Next cut off all the stalks from the base of a bunch of celery. Dip the base in Slick® paint; then carefully print the celery onto the front of the card as many times as desired. Add stems and leaves with Slick® paint. Happy Valentine's Day!

Jennette Shinkle—Child Development Specialist
Bush Early Education Center
Wilmington, DE

Roses are red.
Violets are blue.
Here are some flowers
That I made just for you!
Happy Valentine's Day!

Allison

Face Stamps

Use these face stamps to spread valentine cheer among your little smiling faces! To make one, hot-glue a small wooden heart to a wooden minicandle cup as shown. To use the stamp, use a sponge brush to apply a smooth layer of acrylic paint on the heart. (Acrylic paint does not stain the skin and peels off easily.) Carefully print the heart on a child's face, reminding him not to touch the paint until it has dried. You're sure to see some "heart-y" grins among your students with this idea!

Dayle Timmons—Preschool
Alimacani Elementary
Jacksonville, FL

What's Cookin'?

If you want safe make-believe food cans for your housekeeping area, then try this easy tip. Remove the labels from clean, empty plastic frosting containers. Next carefully peel the labels off fruit, vegetable, and soup cans. Use clear Con-Tact® covering to attach the new labels onto the frosting containers. Now you have safe, realistic-looking food cans for your little chefs!

Brenda Miller—Preschool
Kidecation of Camp Fire
Olean, NY

Handling Valentines

Do you have a supply of paper fruit bags or handled craft bags in your classroom? Use them for valentine mailbags that preschoolers can easily carry. Give each child a personalized bag; then invite him to decorate his bag with stickers, colored glue and glitter, or stamps. Valentine delivery is in the bag!

Susan Pagel—Preschool and Pre-K
St. Paul's Lutheran School
Moline, IL

Toothsome Necklaces

Since February is National Children's Dental Health Month, celebrate with these sparkly tooth necklaces! Mix 1 cup flour, 1/4 cup salt, 1/4 cup clear glitter, and 1/3 cup water; then knead the dough to get out any lumps. Have each child flatten a ball of dough, then shape it into a tooth by making a small dent at the top of the dough with a finger and a bigger dent at the bottom. Make a small hole at the top of each tooth with a drinking straw. Bake the teeth at 250° on a cookie sheet for an hour, or until they are hard. When each tooth has cooled, insert a length of yarn through the hole, and knot the ends to complete the necklace. Your students will be all smiles!

A Tissue, A Tasket, A Basket!

A-tisket, a-tasket, let's make a special basket! Collect an empty, square tissue box for each basket. To make one basket, cut the top off a box. Provide glue and an assortment of artificial flowers, ribbon, lace, rickrack, and buttons for decorating the basket. When the glue has dried, fill the basket with Easter grass and candy, or line it with foil to hold flowers or plants. These baskets are perfect for Easter, May Day, or Mother's Day gifts!

Patricia Duncan—Pre-K And Gr. K
American School For The Deaf
West Hartford, CT

Overheard

Pssst! Chances are that you've heard your little ones say some pretty funny and interesting things! Publish those quotes in a section of your class newsletter titled "Overheard." This section is guaranteed to become parents' favorite part of the newsletter!

Sharon K. Swenson—Preschool And Gr. K
Hazel Lake Montessori
Staples, MN

Fluffy Fabric Bunnies

Help your preschoolers make these adorable bunnies this spring! To make one, place an eight-inch square of thin fabric, wrong side up, on a flat surface. Place a coin in the center; then put two or three small cotton balls on top of the coin. Next fold one corner into the center of the fabric; then repeat with the opposite corner. Roll the fabric from folded corner to folded corner so that you have a long, narrow roll. Thread both ends through a large wooden bead; then fluff the resulting rabbit ears. Finally, use a permanent marker to draw a bunny face on the bead.

Diane White—Preschool, Rotary Youth Centre
Burlington, Ontario, Canada

Jelly Bean Flip Book

Youngsters will flip when they are able to read this sweet book on their own! Draw a rabbit on the top half of a sheet of paper. Write the provided sentence on the paper, spacing it as shown. Duplicate a class supply of the page onto white construction paper. For each child, draw a jelly bean outline on each of a number of 1" x 8 1/2" strips. Staple the same number of strips into place between the lines of text on each page. To complete his book, have each child color the bunny and then color each of the jelly beans a different color. Label the strips. As a variation, make this a counting book by modifying the sentence and programming the strips with sets of jelly beans and matching numerals.

Helen B. Kinser—Preschool And Gr. 1
Crosswell Drive Elementary School, Sumter, SC

Bunny Rabbit found a green jelly bean hiding in the grass.

Organization On The Spot

Here's a tip to instantly organize valuable notes and ideas during teacher workshops. When you hear an idea you want to use, jot it on an index card and write the category (centers, circle time, and so forth) in a top corner. File the cards behind the appropriate heading in a file box. When you return to school, your new ideas will be organized and ready to use!

Julie Plowman—Preschool
Adair Care For Children
Adair, IA

Balloon Blossoms

Use balloons to give these flowers pizzazz! To make one, inflate a small balloon; then tie it to a straw or balloon stick. Glue glitter onto a large, construction-paper flower cutout. When the glue is dry, cut a small slit in the center of the flower; then slip the straw through the slit. Tape two construction-paper leaves near the ends of a pipe cleaner; then twist the pipe cleaner around the straw. These large, sparkly flowers are just the thing to welcome spring!

Carol Rosell, Vineland, NJ

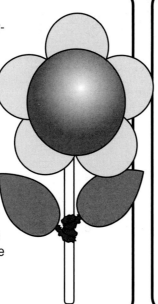

Footprint Butterflies

In years to come, these fluttering footsteps will provide parents with a happy reminder of days when their children were small. Draw a butterfly body in the center of a piece of copy paper; then write the phrases shown. Duplicate a copy for each child. To complete a butterfly, have a child remove his shoes. Place the paper over the soles; then have him rub over the soles with the side of a crayon to create the wings. Encourage each child to give his footprint butterfly to a loved one.

Beth Lemke—Pre-K
Heights Head Start
Coon Rapids, MN

Please keep these footprints
To remind you when I'm tall,
That once I was quite little,
And my feet were also small.

Handy-Dandy Caterpillar

Youngsters will enthusiastically lend a hand to create this adorable caterpillar display! Provide each child with paints and sponges, brushes, cotton swabs, and other creative tools with which to paint a paper circle. Next trace each child's hands onto construction paper; then cut them out. Help each child glue her hand cutouts to the bottom of her circle; then write her first name on the first hand cutout and her last name on the second hand cutout. Mount the circles together with a construction-paper head to create a colorful, cooperative caterpillar.

Keitha-Lynn Stewart—Four-Year-Olds, Little Kids Day Care, Sissonville, WV

"Bee-utiful" Board

Create a bulletin board youngsters will buzz over! Mount a large bee character onto a bulletin board; then surround the bee with close-up shots of your students. Title the board "[Teacher's name]'s 'Bee-utiful' Class." When you change the board, give each child his photo as a keepsake.

Ellen Marston
St. Mary Elementary School
Mobile, AL

Alphabet Mobiles

Use ceiling space to teach the alphabet! Make a large posterboard cutout of each alphabet letter. As each letter is introduced, have youngsters cut out magazine pictures of objects beginning with that letter. Invite each child to share her pictures during circle time; then glue the pictures to the letter cutout. When the letter collage is dry, suspend it from the ceiling. For a five-minute filler, give directions such as, "Everyone hop under the *H*" or "Point to the *P*."

Tracey Dawson—Four-Year-Olds
Loving And Learning
Charleston, SC

Pop-Bottle Art

Put empty, plastic soda bottles to use with this flower-printing activity! Set out several different-sized bottles, corks, and shallow pans of tempera paint. Invite each child to dip the bottom of a bottle into paint, then press it onto a large sheet of paper to print flower shapes. Use small corks to print flower centers. Paint stems and leaves as desired. Now that's pop art!

Vicki Rhonemus—Preschool
Bentonville Preschool
Bentonville, OH

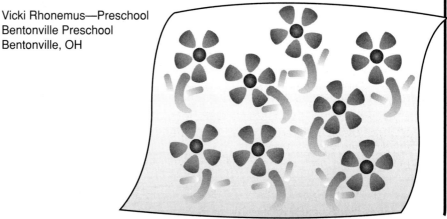

Our Readers Write

"Hand" Towels

These nifty beach towels will have your young ones drying off "with class"! In advance, have each child bring in a large, white bath towel. Enlist volunteers to help each student use fabric paint to make a handprint on every towel. Then use dimensional paint to label each print with the child's name. After adding your own handprint and name to each towel, write the year and your school's name on each one. Allow the paint to dry completely; then send your youngsters home with these wonderful class reminders!

Tina Springs, Main Street Methodist Preschool
Kernersville, NC

Fingerprinted Flowerpots

Thank your room mothers, volunteers, or student teachers with this fabulous fingerprint pot! Have each student use acrylic craft paint to fingerprint a critter on a clay flowerpot. Then use paint pens to label each child's print. When the fingerprints are dry, have students use the pens to add details to their critters. After spraying the pot with clear sealer, plant some flowers in it for the lucky recipient.

Barbara Meyers
Fort Worth Country Day
Fort Worth, TX

If You Give Your Class A Cookie...

Here's a sweet literacy activity that will also help foster friendship and cooperation. Have students bring in boxes and wrappers from cookie packages they have at home. Examine the packaging material with your students, pointing out brand names or other words such as *cookies* or *chips.* Have students create a cookie collage by cutting apart the packages and gluing the pictures and words onto a piece of bulletin-board paper cut to resemble a cookie. As your little ones work to create the collage, encourage them to discuss with each other their favorite cookies. Hang the completed collage in your room; then serve several types of the cookies depicted in the collage as a special treat!

Barbara Kennedy, Epworth Preschool, Indianapolis, IN

Shavuot Bouquets

Decorate a Shavuot table with this tasty cookie bouquet. Use a cookie cutter to cut flower shapes from sugar-cookie dough. Arrange the shapes on a baking pan, allowing enough room to insert a wooden skewer into the side of each flower. Make egg paint by mixing eggs and food coloring—using one egg for each desired color. Lightly brush each cookie with the paint; then bake the cookies. When the cookies are cool, insert the skewers into a block of Styrofoam® that has been inserted into a flowerpot. Place this scrumptious arrangement on a table and let the festivities begin!

Mimi Blumenkrantz—Four-Year-Olds
Yeshiva Shaarei Tzion
Highland Park, NJ

Preschool Days Poem

If you have an end-of-the-year ceremony, have your class recite this poem to the audience. If desired, mount a copy of the poem and a class photo onto paper for each child to take home as a preschool keepsake.

Now I know my ABCs,
Colors, shapes, and days.
I sang some songs,
Learned some poems, rhymes, and fingerplays.
I played outside on sunny days
And inside when it rained.
My little hands and little feet were busy every day.
My teacher was [teacher's name].
I kept her on her toes.
She tied my shoes, combed my hair, and even wiped my nose.
But now it's time to say "Good-bye"
To all my preschool friends.
School is over, summer's here,
But learning never ends!

Mary Hedman—Four-Year-Olds
Clayton, NC